Shmirshky

Shmirshky

the pursuit of
hormone happiness

by E

voice

HYPERION | NEW YORK

Library of Congress Cataloging-in-Publication Data

E (Ellen Sarver Dolgen).
   Shmirshky : the pursuit of hormone happiness / by E. — 1st ed.
       p.   cm.
   Includes bibliographical references.
   ISBN 978-1-4013-4168-8
   1. Menopause—Popular works.   2. Perimenopause—Popular works.   I. Title.
   RG186.E2 2010
   618.1'75—dc22

                                                    2010040075

Hyperion books are available for special promotions and premiums. For details contact the HarperCollins Special Markets Department in the New York office at 212-207-7528, fax 212-207-7222, or email spsales@harpercollins.com.

Interior design and layout inspired by the interior design and layout for *Shmirshky: think inside the box* by Marika van Adelsberg and Joe Gannon, Mulberry Tree Press, Inc.

FIRST EDITION

10   9   8   7   6   5   4   3   2   1

no skipping pages

I made this book short and easy, but if you skip ahead, you will not know a shmirshky from an erlick!

to my bff

My BFF (Birthday Friend Forever), Marcia, whom I first heard use the words *shmirshky* and *erlick*, was an amazing woman. She was vivacious, chic, and endlessly loving. In 2002, Marcia was diagnosed with cancer at the age of seventy-two. Toward the end of her battle, she was home with amazing hospice care. It was her birthday. I wasn't sure what to do. Should I celebrate it or not mention it? I knew it would be the last birthday of her life.

We decided that it was the perfect time to celebrate. I will never forget that October day. When we arrived at Marcia's condo, we were told not to go into her bedroom, but instead were directed to the living room. This was odd; usually we found ourselves flopped on her bed talking and reminiscing about happier times.

Today was different. Marcia was wheeled out with a huge smile on her face. We hadn't seen her out of bed in several months, so this was an amazing sight. We showered her with presents that she immediately wrapped herself up in, and just for a moment, she looked like she was ready to go to a party. Boy, did she love to party!

Marcia was very weak, but her eyes sparkled and her smile was big and beautiful. I still see her in my mind. With joy in her eyes, she left us one last monumental piece of wisdom: *make every day your birthday*. Her message was so powerful; I felt it in my soul. Those of us in the room will never forget it.

With Marcia's wisdom in mind, my friends and I will sometimes randomly send each other a birthday cake. When I receive one on a day that's not my birthday, I feel loved. Simply hearing "Happy Birthday!" makes me joyful and lighthearted, especially when I'm going through a tough time.

Thank you, my dear sweet BFF. Your spirit and wisdom have helped me through many hard days and lonely nights.

shmirshky flow

meet the shmirshky

Got a vagina? Know someone who does? If you don't have one yourself, odds are you have a wife, girlfriend, mother, grandmother, mother-in-law, sister, daughter, friend, mentor, co-worker, or boss who's got one. Vaginas are everywhere!

Vagina, vagina, vagina. What a strange word! It's a word you only hear doctors and awkward sex-education instructors using. All the women I know call it something completely different. My BFF,* Marcia, called the vagina *shmirshky* (pronounced *shmersh-key*) and the penis *erlick* (rhymes with *her-lick*). I love these names! I use them not only to refer to specific parts of a person's anatomy but also the respective sexes that possess them. All women both have and are shmirshkies, and all men have and are erlicks.

I am a shmirshky, a shmirshky who has struggled with perimenopause and menopause. I'm not crazy about these terms either. What a mouthful. Let's call perimenopause PM and menopause M. I like to call this entire time in our lives PM&M! That reminds me of something sweet and wonderful—way more fun.

---

* Birthday Friend Forever

Now you can have a serious and private discussion about menopause, vaginas, and penises and no one within earshot will have a clue what you're talking about. For all they know, you could be talking about a great restaurant or the friends you had drinks with the night before. I once threw a party with *shmirshky* and *erlick* monogrammed on the cocktail napkins. Marcia and I laughed hysterically all night long as the other guests tried to figure out what this meant. Eventually, we told everyone and all laughed together. Welcome to the PM&M, shmirshky, and erlick secrets!

⁀ ⁀

There are over six and a half billion people in the world, and about *half* of them are shmirshkies! By the end of 2008, around fifty million American shmirshkies reached M. That's approximately 18 percent of the U.S. population. And by 2010, nearly *two thirds* of the adult female population in the United States reached age forty or older. That's a lot of shmirshkies in PM&M.*

Since I'm not a doctor, researcher, or scientist, I don't have professional expertise to recommend or not recommend different remedies and procedures. I do, however, have a shmirshky and have experienced PM&M firsthand. I know how hard it can be.

I began writing this book because I was afraid to talk with people about my experience (and I really love to talk!). So the computer became my friend. I'd sit down in the morning in my

---

* I'd love to see the census people knocking on doors asking shmirshkies if they are in PM&M. Most common response: door slam.

bathrobe, with a cup of coffee, and sometimes finish late at night with a martini. All the while, I was chatting away with my computer about PM&M.

shmirshky party alert!

Y Eventually I worked up the courage to invite my girlfriends over for a drink and began talking about my experiences. I found that throwing a little Shmirshky Party is a great way to share and hear stories with the shmirshkies in our lives. I'm including some of those stories in the pages that follow (Shmirshky Party Alerts!). These girlfriend stories are good reminders of how powerful and helpful the sisterhood can be when we share information and support each other.✢

When you're in PM&M, you've got to think *inside* the box! That means think about how you feel, listen to your body, and recognize your needs. When I think inside the box, I'm prioritizing and trusting myself as a shmirshky. Sometimes the erlicks need to think inside the box as well (albeit in a different way than they usually do).

✢ Shmirshky Parties are the best! Have the gals over for cocktails, laughter, and love. You can visit shmirshky.com to find fun tips for your next Shmirshky Party!

Once I started to think inside the box, I realized I had a whole lot to say, so I've turned my writings, research, and conversations into this small book with a BIG story, so my daughter, my friends, the Sisterhood of Shmirshkies, and the erlicks in their lives can all have an easier time with PM&M. I know you're crazy busy, but you can read this while getting your hair done, in between meetings, on the potty, on a plane, at your desk, in a doctor's waiting room, on your cell phone, or in between carpooling your kids.

To help make this little book nice and easy to read, I included some "tickle-your-feet notes." They are kind of like footnotes, but way more fun. This way, you won't have to flip to the back of the book to get fun facts and definitions. For more detail and easy reference, there are a bunch of resources and citations in the back of the book along with a list of Shmirshky Fun Terms and Shmirshky Not-So-Fun Terms.

Okay, enough housekeeping, I think we're ready to jump right in. Be sure to hold on to your shmirshky—you erlicks are always holding yours—and let's get started!

a simpler shmirshky

When I was fourteen, all I wanted was to get my period. My girlfriends got theirs years before I did. They also had boobs. Apparently, I stepped out of the boob line for a minute and missed my allocation. I was probably in the cupcake or raw cookie dough line. (Thank God for the padded bra.)

I became obsessed with getting my period. After all, when you had your period, you were "in," and more important, you got excused from taking a shower in PE. Standing in the shower with a soaking wet towel plastered over my *flat* chest while trying to camouflage my raging embarrassment was no day at the beach. The anticipation of taking that communal shower each day twisted my stomach into knots. I badly needed to be excused. So one day, I woke up and decided that it was time to take action. It was time to fake my period.

Every week, I walked confidently up to my PE teacher and announced that I needed to be excused. Unfortunately, I really didn't understand the menstrual cycle; all I knew was that I wanted a period and the boobs that came with it. Eventually, my teacher pulled me aside to tell me I could only be excused for one week every twenty-eight days. I had overused my excuses!

I solved this problem by copying a friend's period cycle. Whenever she got her period, I pretended to get mine. This worked great, but I still had period envy for almost two years.

Then, one day, it actually came! I was sixteen years old. The fabulous period had arrived, and I was sure that I was going to be "in" now. I knew guys would start flocking around me. I was ecstatic. I had been dreaming of this day for such a long time.

I reached into my purse and pulled out my *longing-to-be-used* belt and pad. (Yes, we had belts in those days, and I don't mean Gucci.) The pad I carried in my purse for years was all shriveled up and yucky. (For you erlicks, this was similar to the condom you carried around when you were fourteen, hoping at any minute that you would get laid.) I put on my belt and pad and waited to feel something magical, something extraordinary—even orgasmic!

As I left the bathroom, my head was pounding and I was still waiting. There was no euphoria. The only thing exploding was my pulsating headache. Did I really have to walk around with blood dripping between my legs onto this huge barge in my crotch for seven days every month of my life? Was *this* what I had been praying for? Are you *kidding* me? By the way, what about those cramps and the pulling on the inside of my thighs? What's up with that? I looked down at my breasts. It was clear that I still didn't need a bra; a couple of Band-Aids would have done the job just fine. A loud, angry voice inside my head kept yelling, "*Hey, where are my boobs? I thought this was a package deal!*"

∽ ∾

Do you know any shmirshkies who love getting their periods or look forward to drowning in a sea of raging hormones? Do you know any shmirshkies (or erlicks for that matter) who can't wait for the monthly PMS,* the bloating, the constipation, the cravings, and the sore, exploding breasts? Isn't the emotional roller coaster such a blast? Nearly two weeks out of every month, you and the poor souls around you are stuck in the MTZ (Menstruation Twilight Zone). Not to mention the many hours in your lifetime dedicated to picking out period paraphernalia. Yikes! You've got your heavy, your light, your scented, your long, your wide, your thong, your miniflow, your maxiflow, your gold, your silver, and your bronze. How about the applicators? Cardboard, plastic, environmentally friendly, or the string only. Oh, my favorite is the pad with wings! Wings? I don't want wings when I'm on my period, I want ice cream.

We spend most of our time wondering where our period is, when it's going to come, and when it will go away. It's less like a period and more like a question mark. The only thing consistent about my period was that it always seemed to join my husband and me on our vacations (including our honeymoon!). Of course, everyone wants to take their period with them on vacation, right? I packed it a bag, bought it a pair of sunglasses

---

* PMS (premenstrual syndrome) refers to the symptoms that shmirshkies often get before their period arrives. In addition to what's mentioned above, you may get a headache and feel unusually emotional, irritable, tired, anxious, or depressed, just to name a few. Sounds like fun, right?

and some wings, and off we went. My husband, David, my period, and I have been to many fun places over the past thirty-
four years. It's no wonder that from the moment I first got my
period, I was sure I'd never miss it once it was gone. And why
would I? I figured PM&M would be a piece of cake . . . mmm,
cake!

shmirshky latin

So what the hell is PM&M if not a delicious dessert? Well, if you don't know anything about a subject, the first thing you do is look it up, right? There are lots of long funky words involved in the PM&M experience, so let's see what *Merriam-Webster's Medical Dictionary** can tell us about a few of the key terms (in order of experience):

pre·ma·ture men·o·pause
Pronunciation: ˌprē-mə-ˈchur ˈmən-ə-ˌpȯz
Function: *noun*
: refers to menopause that occurs before the age of forty✚

pre·men·o·pause
Pronunciation: ˌprē-ˈmen-ə-ˌpȯz
Function: *noun*
: the premenopausal period of a woman's life; *especially* : the period of irregular menstrual cycles preceding menopause

---

✱ By permission. From *Merriam-Webster's Medical Dictionary* © 2005 by Merriam-Webster, Incorporated (www.Merriam-Webster.com).
✚ Definition by permission of Dr. Margery Gass, Executive Director, North American Menopause Society.

peri·men·o·pause
Pronunciation: ˌper-ē-ˈmen-ə-ˌpȯz
Function: *noun*
: the period around the onset of menopause that is often marked by various physical signs (as hot flashes and menstrual irregularity)

men·o·pause
Pronunciation: ˈmen-ə-ˌpȯz
Function: *noun*
1 a (1) : the natural cessation of menstruation occurring usually between the ages of 45 and 55 with a mean in Western cultures of approximately 51 (2) : the physiological period in the life of a woman in which such cessation and the accompanying regression of ovarian function occurs—called also *climacteric*—compare PERIMENOPAUSE **b :** cessation of menstruation from other than natural causes (as from surgical removal of the ovaries)

post·men·o·paus·al
Pronunciation: ˌpōst-ˌmen-ə-ˈpȯ-zəl
Function: *adjective*
1 : having undergone menopause <*postmenopausal* women>
2 : occurring after menopause <*postmenopausal* osteoporosis>
- **post·men·o·paus·al·ly** /-ē / *adverb*

Wow, these definitions are soooo simple. It sounds like a breeze. It comes and goes, and you're done! Wouldn't that be nice? Clearly no one checked with Mrs. Webster before printing these definitions. No wonder I thought PM&M would be as easy as pie . . . mmm, pie!

shmirshky alert

As it turns out, PM&M isn't just the simple cessation of a bodily function. It's your brain, your body, and your life transforming into something you're totally unfamiliar with. You begin to question your sanity, relationships, hormones, genetics, sex drive, age, food, clothes, underwear, everything! It's an every day, all day, and all-consuming shmirshky shitstorm.

Here's a little forecast of what this storm might entail: *

✳ You begin worrying that you may be in the early stages of Alzheimer's, ✢ because you can't seem to grab a memory or a thought. You look at your dear friends and children and blank on their names. Your refrigerator and the dashboard of your car are plastered with sticky note reminders.

---

* I wish I could tell you exactly at what age this storm will start to brew, but it's different for every shmirshky. Most shmirshkies begin to experience symptoms in their forties or fifties. Early storms can also occur for some shmirshkies, which in some cases is referred to as premature menopause. You can find more on this in chapter 6, "How to Schedule PM&M."

✢ Alzheimer's disease is a form of dementia. It's a progressive, degenerative brain disease that affects one's capacity for memory and thought.

✳ Your eyes are constantly watering, as the least little thing makes you cry. You find yourself defending this constant dripping by announcing that you have allergies, even if it's the dead of winter and nothing is blooming. In contrast, your shmirshky may be oddly dry.

✳ You are grumpy, unusually depressed, irritable, hypersensitive, have erratic mood swings, and feel lonely, yet all you want is to be alone.

✳ Your periods begin to act weird: they disappear for months at a time, then they either arrive for just a quick second (spotting) or show up big and heavy, as if to say, "I'm baaaaack!"

✳ Your internal thermometer starts to change. You're hot all the time! (This is not the kind of hot that you wake up your lover over.) You often find yourself perspiring as if you just finished a hike in a tropical rainforest, but you've actually been sitting down or just woke up.

✳ You no longer sleep through the night. Instead, you wake up two or three or more times. You might begin to find packages arriving at your doorstep filled with *essential* items bought during late-night shopping sprees: paring knives, food dehydrators, juicers, all-in-one home gyms, weight-loss programs, and magical carpet cleaners, to name a few.

✳ You find yourself staring in the mirror, startled at the changes you see: your skin is dry, randomly breaking out, or looks like it needs to be ironed. (I tried steaming. It doesn't work.)

✳ You start to not feel sexy anymore and find that your significant other has placed a "remember me?" sticky note on his erlick or her shmirshky.

✳ You may feel like you have to pee all the time and/or find that you're having symptoms similar to a urinary tract infection, but you aren't in a new relationship or even having the fun that usually comes *before* the misery.

✳ You can't seem to find a product that lasts longer than a week to cover the gray in your hair. Even your bush is turning gray. Meanwhile, your chin is randomly sprouting extra-long dark hairs (get me the tweezers, please!), and what you haven't waxed, shaved, or lasered off is balding.

✳ You have PMS-like symptoms *every day*. You have cravings and your appetite is insatiable; your body is expanding; your clothes are getting really tight; and you are being a total bitchface!

✳ In addition to all of the above symptoms giving you a big fat headache, you may find that you are having migraine headaches as well.

Do any of these sound familiar? If you group a bunch of them together, you may be at the beginning or smack in the middle of PM&M. Each of us experiences different symptoms and to different degrees of intensity. For a more detailed list of symptoms, take a look at the Shmirshky Daily Symptoms Chart on page 168. It can all be frustrating, confusing, and scary, but don't worry; you are not alone.

the alien and the organizer

I was secretly screaming, "What, what, what is happening to me!?!"

Was I possessed? Did some alien from outer space come down to earth and replace my brain with Play-Doh? My entire personality changed, and I didn't like the new me. I was turning into someone I didn't even want to spend the day with.

I first noticed some changes when I was around forty-eight years old. I was not nearly as energetic as I used to be, and I totally pooped out by mid-afternoon! I often needed to get into a hot bath just to warm up my feet. I couldn't seem to grab thoughts from my brain, and my mind would go blank mid-sentence. I thought about the possibility that I was beginning M, but I quickly concluded that I was way too young for that. I was programmed to think that M = OLD, OLD = WRINKLED, WRINKLED = FEAR! NO NO NO! I would *not* let myself go there. I shoved that thought into a drawer and slammed it shut.

I then began worrying that these were the early signs of Alzheimer's disease or dementia. I did not have time for that either. All my life I had prided myself on being a masterfully organized, multitasking dynamo. I was not ready to lose that part of my personality.

——————— shmirshky party alert!

Nor was my friend Joan. She is an interior decorator with real panache, who began her PM&M storm at the age of forty-four, when she suddenly became very moody and impatient. Joan told me, "I would get angry at the littlest things. I couldn't help myself when something was upsetting to me. I felt like everything had to get done and it had to be done *now*." Even Joan's family and colleagues noticed the change in her behavior (go figure!). The aliens are infiltrating the Sisterhood!

At first, the rush of symptoms can be discombobulating. During this confusion, I was lucky that my special erlick, David, was able to finish my sentences for me. After so many years together, he seemed to know what I was thinking. He sensed that my memory loss was horribly embarrassing to me, so he sweetly mastered subtle ways to feed me facts. It was wonderful and so very kind of him.

I made a habit out of making jokes about my memory loss— I just kept laughing it off. Meanwhile, I threw out all my aluminum pans because I read that aluminum can contribute to

Alzheimer's. I changed my deodorant to a nonaluminum, salt-based brand. I was freaking out, nothing was helping my memory, and to top it all off, my new salty deodorant was not exactly keeping me fresh as a flower. I kept hoping it was just a fluke, and perhaps tomorrow I would wake up sharp as a tack, smelling like roses.

the big shmirshky cover-up

Pushing all these fears aside left me anxious, lonely, and desperate to feel better. Still I kept on pushing. After all, I pushed out two babies; I could certainly push away these bothersome thoughts. I was a happy person, and I was not interested in being sick or "less than." I didn't talk about this with *anyone* because talking about it would make it real. Instead, the voice in my head kept secretly chanting the old-school shmirshky mantra: "I am fine. I am fine. I am fine."

When a shmirshky says she is "fine," this is the first sign of "the cover-up." Yes, we shmirshkies are really good at the cover-up. It's not that we don't want to be honest with those we love, but rather that we aren't honest with ourselves. We're afraid of being less than: less than perfect, less than 100 percent functioning, less than able to juggle it all. I think you get it—"less than" typically doesn't sit well with a shmirshky.

All this cover-up has helped make PM&M a huge secret. I understand that it's way more fun to talk about a new movie, fashion, sex, politics, or food, but we need each other for this one. We need the Sisterhood to help us through. We need our mothers, special aunts, and revered elders to share. When I asked my mother how PM&M was for her, she told me that she didn't have time for it. That was that—end of discussion! I'm reminded that this was the same person who told me never to let a boy touch my thigh until I was married. Word spread pretty fast that I wasn't exactly the hottest date in town.

For some, it can be embarrassing to admit PM&M is challenging and, at times, very depressing. I am here to tell you loud and clear that it *can* be quite difficult. Each shmirshky will have her own journey. Each of our bodies is different, as different as every shmirshky's breasts—no two are alike. This is the challenging part. It's not black and white; it's all gray. I recently read in a fashion magazine that gray is the new black. This brought me no comfort—I yearned for black-and-white answers.

shmirshky party alert!

When I asked Patty if her mom had ever prepared her for PM&M, she responded, "Absolutely not!" Patty told me that her mother never spoke about it and to this day maintains that she never went through menopause. (Trust me, she did go through it!) From Patty's perspective at the time, her mother "simply had a breakdown. She got into her bed one day and stayed there for four years." Patty, a teenager then, stepped in and "kept stuff together," making the holiday dinners as well as the daily lunches for her sister. She used to color her mom's hair once in a while in the hopes that covering the gray would somehow help her mother feel better. Unfortunately, hair dye does not fix PM&M. It must have been so difficult for Patty to be the child *and* the mother at such a young age.

I remember my mom telling me that she had to take a leave of absence from her teaching job to come home and take care of my grandmother when my grandma was around fifty. Apparently my grandma had become very depressed. I never realized what that was all about until recently. Perhaps my grandmother was going through a PM&M depression. Back then, doctors gave people shock treatments for depression, and I wonder if that's what happened to my grandmother. She was a vivacious shmirshky who loved to celebrate life—far from depressed. But even the most spirited shmirshkies can drift into a depressed state during PM&M. I wanted to reach back in time to hug my grandmother and tell her I understood exactly how she felt.

After hearing that, I totally realized why my mom didn't have time for PM&M. Do you blame her after what her mother went through? This is another reason why PM&M became such a secret. Why would women want to talk about what was happening to them if it meant possibly receiving shock treatments as a result? It's no wonder that my mom's favorite saying is "I'm fine, fine, super fine."

shmirshky party alert!

Y My marvelous graphic designer friend Sharon had a grandmother and grandaunts who were institutionalized for a time in their late forties and early fifties. Sharon suspects that this was PM&M-related, although she told me that during her own hardest PM&M moments, the thought of getting locked away in an institution where they "take care of this new you and put you back together" didn't sound so bad! Unfortunately, the older generations of shmirshkies weren't exactly going to Club Med.

Y My extraordinary book maven friend Blanca had a slightly different experience with her mom. She told me, "When my mother was going through it, she let me know it was happening, but I was just too preoccupied with my own life to give a hoot."

It can be jarring when we see our mothers and loved ones suffering. This can lead to a PM&M cover-up in reverse. Sometimes we understand what they are going through and sometimes it's a mystery, but either way, it's our responsibility to acknowledge and educate ourselves about their struggle. This can be easier said than done.

Whole generations of shmirshkies have been involved in the cover-up, and everyone tends to think they have to be "fine." I'm sad that my mother and grandmother handled it all alone. I don't want any more shmirshkies to feel alone. Let's not repeat the years of silently suffering through PM&M. Let's bust open the shmirshky cover-up and sound the alarm for others to think inside the box.

By the way, next time a shmirshky you love says she's "fine," ask her how she *really* feels.

how to schedule PM&M

You can't!

PM&M arrives unscheduled, uninvited, and often sooner than you'd think. The biggest myth about PM&M is that it begins when you're *old*. This is simply NOT TRUE! PM typically begins in your forties, when you're young and active.

PM&M arrives like a baby's first tooth. It breaks through at a different age for each person. Some shmirshkies begin the PM&M process when they're thirty-eight, some when they're forty-eight. There is no right or wrong age for PM&M, and you won't receive a "save the date" to let you know when the festivities will begin.

There's no rhyme or reason to the length of the process either. The perimenopause stage can last six to ten years before you finally hit menopause. Contrary to what many people think, you don't technically hit menopause until you've been period-free for twelve consecutive months. Between the onset of your first symptom and the point at which you hit menopause, there's enough time for bell-bottoms to be in style, go out of style, and then come back in style again.

Regardless of when you begin the perimenopause stage, if

you hit menopause when you're *under the age of forty,* it's generally classified as premature menopause. I know, the word *premature* makes it sound like you started the race before the gun went off. Don't worry; if you are experiencing premature menopause, you won't be thrown into some sort of menopausal doghouse. Premature menopause may occur as a result of one's genetic makeup, an illness, or medical procedures such as a hysterectomy. *

Since there's no magic age for the onset of PM&M, there's no need to feel ashamed or embarrassed about the nature of your symptoms or the timing of their arrival. ⸸

---

* You may come across another term called *early menopause.* Early menopause describes both natural and induced menopause before the age of forty-five, which includes all cases of premature menopause. I hate to be early to a party, personally, but everyone's got their own style! However, there are some resources that don't consider surgically induced menopause before the age of forty to be premature menopause. I know this may be confusing, and you're probably thinking, "Who gives a rat's ass about these definitions? All I want is to feel good." Since these terms are out there in the PM&M world, I do want you to understand what they mean. Knowing where you fit into the PM&M calendar can help you feel calmer and better equipped to work with your doctor.
⸸ Why aren't there any traditions to make this easier? When you turn seven, you take your first Communion; when you turn thirteen, you're bat mitzvahed; when you start throwing cans of soup at your partner, you're in PM&M.

don't hide your shmirshky under a bush

This chapter is not about waxing, laser hair removal, or shaving your shmirshky; it's about preparation. So many shmirshkies pride themselves on being prepared. If you look in our purses, you may find anything from a complete outfit change to a spare tire. Mothers of young children routinely walk around with a whole nursery in their diaper bags and enough hand sanitizer to sterilize an entire country. My mother is ninety years old and still keeps a piece of paper in her purse that lists the day I got my period and all the vaccinations I've had since 1953, just in case. This is the kind of preparation I'm talking about.

The Sisterhood is so prepared and open when it comes to childbearing and child rearing. From pregnancy to college applications, my friends and family were always full of support. One of my favorite pieces of advice was from my friend Melody, who helped prepare me for when my daughter, Sarah, became a teenager. Melody told me that when Sarah hit puberty, she would wake up one day and hate me. I recall looking at my precious little blonde, curly-haired baby girl, age four, dressed in her favorite sparkly pink ballerina outfit with spaghetti stains on it, and somehow, I couldn't imagine that she would ever hate me! How could our relationship ever get to that point? We had so much fun together.

In anticipation of this, I began telling Sarah (when she was a preteen) that someday soon she would more than likely find that she hated me. She was as shocked as I was. I proceeded to explain that it would only be temporary and that she should not feel guilty about these feelings. They were normal for teenage girls. I assured her that I would understand and that she would grow out of it.

When Sarah finally hit her teenage years, I repeatedly asked her, "Do you hate me today?" We'd both laugh. As in any close relationship, tensions did inevitably arise, but thanks to Melody, we were prepared. I can't thank her enough for this wonderful advice.

Of course, you can't avoid PM&M (or mother-daughter animosity) just by being prepared. However, if you're busy hiding from your shmirshky and the challenges of PM&M, then you will not be equipped to handle what may lie ahead. Here are a few things to keep in your PM&M Prep Kit: sticky notes; tweezers; a hand fan; a lot of patience, love, and support; and a tampon (trust me). Remember the Girl Scout motto: "Be prepared."

sleepless in PM&M

For the first half of my life I was a great sleeper. If they gave out gold medals for sleeping, I would have been adorned with them. On a plane, a subway, a bus, a car, or during a boring speech, if I was tired I would nod off into a wonderful sleep. Often on the car ride home from dinner parties, my friends would take bets on how long it would be before my chin began its descent into my chest. Thank goodness drooling was not part of this act.

Suddenly, my gold medals flew off and I became sleepless. Yearning to be "fine," I dismissed these sleepless nights as fluke occurrences. Maybe I was stressed, maybe I had eaten too much, drunk too much, or not exercised enough.

Still, night after night I found myself unable to sleep. Often I would fall asleep, then wake up around 3:00 A.M., unable to fall back to sleep. Other nights I would toss and turn, dozing for an hour or two at a time. I was so tired, but I couldn't sleep. It was torturous.

I love the movie *Sleepless in Seattle*, but sleepless in PM&M is neither cute nor romantic. My nights became one big nightmare: lonely, depressing, and exhausting. Instead of jumping out of bed in the morning with a smile, I found myself struggling to function. Along with my sleepless nights came incredible mood swings, random tears, and an MIA sex life. (See the Shmirshky Daily Symptoms Chart on page 168.) David and I were both worried about me and our relationship. Was this going to be our life together from now on?

————————— shmirshky party alert!

Y My friend Debbi's Olympic-quality sleeping habits came to a halt one night when she suddenly felt hot, boiling hot! Debbi's experience was like getting stuck outside during a record heat wave surrounded by hundreds of people with no room to move. Her heat rush was routinely followed by a downpour of sweat resulting in a soaking-wet nightgown, drenched sheets, a chill, and plenty of anxiety. These sweat sessions kept her and her husband up at night, with a pile of laundry rising alongside their bed and no sleep in sight. Oh joy!

Y Patty had a similar experience. She would lie awake at night, soaking wet, staring at the ceiling. She was so hot, she felt like she had to inch away from her husband. Maybe Patty should have worn a sign that read DANGER: DO NOT TOUCH THE SLEEPLESS SHMIRSHKY.

A 2008 study done by researchers at the University of Arizona College of Nursing found that the #1 biggest problem for shmirshkies entering M (94.5 percent of the shmirshkies in this study!) was sleep deprivation. So, although I *felt* totally alone, clearly I was far from the only shmirshky experiencing this symptom. Next time you can't sleep, instead of counting sheep, try counting sleep-deprived PM&M shmirshkies.

the thyroidian slip

It's true that PM&M can be pretty complicated. To make it even more confusing, *some* shmirshkies find that when the PM&M storm starts to brew, it goes from rain to sleet with the onset of a thyroid condition.* It can be difficult to differentiate a thyroid condition from PM&M because some of the symptoms are very similar: nervousness, irritability, fatigue, depression, difficulty sleeping, night sweats, and changes in menstrual patterns, to name a few. Often, shmirshkies brush off thyroid imbalance symptoms as part of their PM&M experience. Don't make this mistake! You can have serious health issues if you leave a thyroid condition untreated.

(Don't stop reading, baby! There's more thyroid info on the next page, but I'm keeping all the footnotes on their proper pages so you don't have to flip back and forth. Odds are, you're already flipping out as it is!)

---

* Thyroid conditions affect the thyroid gland, which is a small, two-lobed gland in your neck that uses iodine to make thyroid hormones that help regulate your metabolism.

Thyroid conditions come in two common forms: hyper-thyroidism* and hypothyroidism.✢ Are you a hyper/hypo? Be sure to get your TSH✕ levels checked to find out (see chapter 14, "Shmirshky Numbers"). Also check to see if anyone in your family has a thyroid condition, as it can be hereditary. I know what you're thinking—PM&M is quite the handful all by itself, give me a break already with this thyroid business! Believe me, you're preaching to the choir. Bear with me for just a bit while I walk you through the experiences of my friend and me so you can see how important it is to proactively manage your own health.

At my yearly physical exam, my doctor announced that I had Hashimoto's disease.✛ I thought, "What in the world is

---

* Hyperthyroidism, or an overactive thyroid gland, is usually caused by the autoimmune illness called Grave's disease. In this condition, the body's immune system produces an antibody that stimulates the gland to make an excess amount of T3 and T4, the two forms of thyroid hormone. (By the way, the 3 and the 4 refer to the number of iodines in that form of the hormone.) If you're a "hyper," you may experience some of these symptoms: enlarged thyroid gland (goiter), bulging eyes, sudden weight loss, rapid heartbeat, increased appetite, nervousness and anxiety, irritability, tremor in the hands and fingers, sweating, changes in menstrual patterns, increased sensitivity to heat, more frequent bowel movements, and difficulty sleeping.

✢ In hypothyroidism, the thyroid gland doesn't produce enough thyroid hormone, which slows down the body's metabolism. If you're a "hypo," you may experience weight gain, increased sensitivity to cold, dry skin and hair, slow pulse, low blood pressure, constipation, depressed mood, muscle aches/weakness, hair loss, low energy, and all kinds of sluggishness. It is usually caused by Hashimoto's disease (see below). Studies show that by the time shmirshkies hit age fifty, one out of every ten to twelve has some degree of hypothyroidism. By age sixty, it's one shmirshky out of every five or six.

✕ TSH stands for thyroid stimulating hormone. An imbalance in your TSH levels is one of the main indicators of a thyroid condition.

✛ Hashimoto's disease is also called chronic lymphocytic thyroiditis. The immune system attacks the thyroid gland, which causes inflammation and leads to an underactive thyroid (hypothyroidism).

that?" The name sounded like a breakfast cereal, a rare butterfly, or something I would yell before I tried to chop a block in half with my bare hands. The word *disease* really bothered me too. I couldn't imagine that I had a disease. No way, no how!

This *new* doctor pointed out that over the past five years, my blood test results had shown that my TSH was way too high. I was shocked. He gave me the name of an endocrinologist✿ to go see about my thyroid. I didn't research the doctor or question this referral in any way before making an appointment with him (big mistake), but I *did* rush home from my physical so that I could Google Hashimoto's disease and thyroid conditions.

The hypo symptoms were me to a T, especially the increased sensitivity to cold. Wow! For years, I had complained to my previous doctor that my hands and feet were constantly cold. He continually told me not to worry, that I just had poor circulation. I cannot believe that I walked out of his office every year comfortable with that answer, comfortable living with freezing feet. Since when was bigmouth me such a wallflower? Remember, shmirshkies are great at the cover-up. To problem-solve, I covered up my freezing dogs with the heaviest, warmest thermal socks I could find. I even wore those beauties to bed every night. Did I mention I lived in Arizona at the time? I know what you're thinking: who wears thermal socks to bed when it's 110° outside? All I can say is thank goodness David didn't have a foot fetish!

✿ An endocrinologist is a medical expert specializing in the diseases of the endocrine system (glands and hormones). Thank God for these doctors!

In my research, I learned that it is recommended for anyone with a thyroid imbalance to have a yearly ultrasound scan* of the thyroid gland in order to detect nodules that may have gone unnoticed by a physical exam. These nodules can be cancerous. This was an important test, and I wanted to be sure not to forget to ask for it.

I arrived at the specialist's office with my ultrasound sticky note in hand. He did a physical exam of my thyroid gland and said he was going to put me on medicine that would bring my TSH back down to normal. I told him that I wanted to have an ultrasound of my thyroid as well, but he insisted I didn't need one because he didn't feel any nodules. I guess he thought he had magic hands, but that wasn't going to cut it for me. I stressed that I was very proactive about my health and wanted the scan as a precaution, thank you. My gut told me to get this test. This was (and still is) *my* body and *I* get to decide! He was very annoyed with me, but I wasn't leaving his office without an order slip for the scan.

Guess what the test results revealed? I had a nodule on my left thyroid lobe. It took great restraint for me not to tell him where he could shove those *magic hands*.

If you're intimidated by your doctor, find yourself unusually afraid to speak up, or feel you're not being heard and respected, then consider finding another doctor. Remember to listen to your gut and *do not* settle. Do not be afraid to change your doctor. It's not like getting a divorce; a lawyer is not required.

---

* Ultrasound uses high-frequency sound waves to take pictures of the internal systems of the body. There is no exposure to radiation. You don't feel a thing!

Needless to say, I found a new endocrinologist, one who is very well respected in the medical world, conservative, and a good listener. After a biopsy and eventually surgery, we discovered that the nodule was benign.✢ Still, I have to stay on my meds to keep my thyroid balanced.

─────────────── shmirshky party alert!

Y Maria's mother and two sisters all have hyperthyroidism✻ (remember, your susceptibility can be hereditary), and when she told me about her sister's traumatic experience, my heart just sank. "My forty-five-year-old sister was in such denial about her symptoms that she waited to get help until she was unable to carry her groceries up to her apartment without resting in between steps. Unfortunately, she waited so long that—along with other permanent long-term side effects like hair loss and bulging eyes—she suffered heart damage and needed a valve replacement." The consequences of the "I'm fine" mentality can be severe and sometimes irreversible.

Even after her sister's traumatic experience, Maria didn't associate her own symptoms with what her sister

---

✢ Some shmirshkies find that they do have thyroid cancer, but in many cases it's a very treatable cancer.
✻ Yep, Maria was a hyper (*not* a hypo, like me). This means she had an overactive thyroid, which is usually caused by the autoimmune illness called Grave's disease.

had gone through. At forty-four, Maria started experiencing a huge metabolism shift. She lost thirty pounds in six weeks—can you believe that? She suffered from extreme fatigue, a racing heart, and tremendous night sweats. Maria was accustomed to swimming one hundred laps a day, and suddenly she was struggling to catch her breath after just one. She thought she might be experiencing PM&M symptoms and was determined to be "fine," but as the days progressed she became increasingly edgy, paranoid, and angry. She just couldn't live like that anymore.

After eight weeks of suffering, Maria finally broke through the cover-up and called a doctor. (Hallelujah!) With the help of a wonderful endocrinologist, she was diagnosed with hyperthyroidism, received radioactive iodine treatment (RAI), and is now on thyroid medication, which requires periodic monitoring. Thankfully, Maria was properly diagnosed before any permanent consequences set in.

Dramatic hyper/hypo stories are common among PM&M shmirshkies. If it doesn't affect you, odds are it is affecting a shmirshky you know and love. Ultimately, we all have to take responsibility for our own well-being. Learn your family history and get yourself in to see a doctor if you are experiencing persistent symptoms.

not-so-hot flashes

As my thyroid numbers improved, I thought for sure that I'd be fine. Yes, being "fine" was my main goal. I didn't have cold feet anymore (I was sockless!), and my energy level was much better, but I still couldn't think clearly, nor was I sleeping well. In addition, new symptoms gradually began cropping up, or, should I say, dripping all over the place. I was hot!

I began perspiring in strange places. Let me tell you, I will never forget my first flash. It was not hot outside; in fact, it was a beautiful spring day and I was wearing a lightweight pantsuit. All of a sudden, I felt a flush of heat come over me. When I rose from my chair, I noticed that something wet was dripping down the inner seam of my pants leg! No, I did not pee in my pants. I was perspiring! I am not kidding. Thank goodness I always carry a big purse. (I think big purses make my hips look smaller.) With my purse firmly planted in front of my shmirshky, I ran to my car. I looked down in utter disbelief. What in the world was this? Did I have a perspiring shmirshky? Did my shmirshky sneak off to the gym for a quick 5K while I wasn't looking? I started signing my e-mails "HS (Hot Shmirshky) OMG!" Was I the only "HS" in the world?

It was getting a lot harder to deny that I was in PM. It was sort of like getting stuck in the rain and telling people that it's still sunny outside. You're soaking wet—no one's buying it! My body was dragging me into PM&M, and I did not want to go.

One of the reasons I was able to stay in denial for so long was that I didn't fully understand the sweaty symptoms of PM&M. I thought a PM&M hot flash happened when a shmirshky's face got suddenly flushed. That is true for some, but not for others. While most PM&M shmirshkies get hot flashes in one way or another, we all experience them differently. We are a hot group! Some shmirshkies get them during the day, while others get night sweats. Some shmirshkies get them on their upper body, while others (like me) get them on their lower body. They can range from quick flashes of heat to super sweat sessions like the ones my friends Debbi and Patty endured (see chapter 8, "Sleepless in PM&M").

———————— shmirshky party alert!

One of my dearest Gay Husbands,* Paul, told me a story about a business trip he was on to Switzerland in the dead of winter. One of his brilliant

———————————————————————————

* I love my Gay Husbands! This is someone who not only gives you all the love and support of a husband but also enjoys shopping and getting mani-pedis, and knows how to throw a fabulous party.

biotech executives was seated next to him when suddenly beads of sweat began dripping down her face. She was glistening in the reading light. Immediately, she began peeling off layers of clothes, one piece after another, until she was down to a sleeveless T-shirt. Later, during a highly sophisticated presentation to a Swiss venture capitalist, the dreaded flash appeared again. This woman did not strip down to her T-shirt during the presentation—though Paul was sort of afraid that she might—and not a word was spoken about the flash, as PM&M was definitely not on the meeting's agenda.

What's a business shmirshky to do? Well, many PM&M shmirshkies find it helpful to pack an extra shirt or even a fresh outfit in their purse or briefcase. This might seem silly, but if you're stuck in the Alps in the middle of winter and you're sweating like it's New Orleans in August, you'll be glad you brought along a change of clothes.

On the return flight home, Paul turned to his coworker and said, "You know you're in menopause, right?" They talked about PM&M extensively and he offered his support. (Paul is quite familiar with the topic thanks to his Straight Wife—that's me!) Good for Paul for putting PM&M on the agenda.

Sharon told me that she doesn't have hot flashes— she has night sweats. As any of the sleepless

PM&Mers in chapter 8 would predict, Sharon would trade her night sweats for a flash in a flash! Without warning, she wakes up in the middle of the night covered in sweat. The first time it happened, she thought she had experienced a "great sex dream" but just couldn't remember it. She made herself go right back to sleep, hoping she could plug back in to the orgasmic dream. It never happened. The next day Sharon shared her "sex dream" experience with her girlfriend, who was trying not to laugh as she explained to Sharon that this was "no dream, honey," it was PM&M.

My friend Lisa, age fifty-three, has a sexy new boyfriend. One night, after making passionate love, Lisa curled up in his arms, dozed off, and then suddenly felt hot—as she put it, "I know I'm 'hot,' but I also felt like I had a really bad sunburn." She was "WET, soaking wet," under her breasts and between her legs. The bed was soaking wet as well. She jumped out of bed, thinking she had urinated in her sleep. Lisa stood there, mortified, wondering how she was going to tell her new boyfriend that she had peed in his bed. It took her a few minutes to realize what had actually transpired, and in the morning she told her boyfriend about the incident. The first thing he said was, "YUK." Lisa agreed, and they discussed the situation openly. I'm so proud of Lisa and her boyfriend for talking about this and not letting it get in the way of tearing each other's clothes off. *

Everyone's experience is different. Some PM&M shmirshkies find that when they drink alcohol or hot beverages such as coffee and tea, their hot flashes are hotter and their sleep is even more restless! Of course, we all know that when you drink, you seem to eat more. This is not good for the already ever-expanding PM&M shmirshky. Don't freak out too much, though, as not every shmirshky has sensitivities to alcohol. Thank goodness, because cocktail hour helps some shmirshkies open up and talk about PM&M, instead of hiding under that bush.

Ultimately, it was these not-so-hot flashes that forced me out of hiding. I had to admit to myself that I was dealing with more than just a thyroid condition; I was beginning PM&M. That's when my problem solving kicked into high gear.

---

* Who says there can't be a sexy story in a menopause book?

shmirshky in the basement

I needed to read more about PM&M, and fast! So where does the layperson go for help? (What a funny term! The last thing I was thinking of was laying anyone!) Books are a great place to start. Some of them are hundreds of pages long. They can be very technical, very medical, and there aren't any hot romance scenes to keep you awake. Keep reading anyway. This research is critical to understanding what's happening to your body and will help ensure that you can communicate well with your doctor in order to successfully manage your own PM&M journey.*

My first shmirshky recon trip was at a wonderful neighborhood bookstore. I walked all over the store looking for books on PM&M, but I couldn't find a thing! Then I saw the basement. Yes, you guessed it—the PM&M section was in the basement. I guess PM&M is not cool or chic enough to be on the first floor. I couldn't find any PM&M books on the Employees' Picks table either. Shocker. I dragged myself downstairs and gathered as many books as I could hold (FYI,

---

* There are so many books to choose from, and new ones arrive on the market all the time. Sift through the options and find the books that work for you.

there are no stairs to deal with when you buy online!). As I stumbled back up to the cashier, I noticed that she was a young shmirshky. She gaped at me as she rang up over a dozen books on PM&M. I told her that I would read them all and let her know how it went. She laughed. I thought, oh man, you just wait.

shmirshky private "i"

It didn't take long before I realized that I needed to find a great gynecologist who specialized in PM&M to help me with my sweat-stravaganza. Finding the right PM&M specialist is critical. This might not be the same doctor who delivered your babies or does your routine Pap smear. You may need to dig a little deeper to find a PM&M specialist who's right for you.

This shouldn't be too hard. After all, shmirshkies are gatherers; we know how to find what we're looking for, whether it's a cute new top or the perfect gift for a friend. Unfortunately, many shmirshkies spend more time researching hotels, hairdressers, and restaurants than researching doctors. Have you ever chosen a doctor because he or she is close to your house? I know I have, yet I never simply picked the closest hotel to my destination; I would drive miles out of my way for the most fabulous place to stay. Remember, you've got to think inside the box! Use your finely tuned investigative skills to find a great PM&M specialist. Here are some tips to gathering good doctor recommendations (you can search later for a delicious bite to eat nearby):

✳ If you know a great doctor who excels in his or her specific field, this is an excellent place to start. Great doctors often know other great doctors, and receptionists and office managers can usually get a recommendation for you. If you like your current gynecologist, ask him or her to recommend a PM&M specialist. There might be someone right there in the same office who specializes in PM&M.

✳ Ask trustworthy friends and family for recommendations. I keep an ongoing list of different doctors who people recommend to me. Start keeping your own list, and then you'll be a good resource for your friends as well!

✳ Go online. The Internet is a massive medical resource. You can start by taking a look at the North American Menopause Society's resources for finding a "Certified Menopause Practitioner." Just follow these links for more information:
http://www.menopause.org/compexam.aspx
http://www.menopause.org/referralservice.aspx

✳ If you happen to know a medical student, or know someone who does, pick his or her brain. Medical students often interact with a lot of doctors and might know of some great doctors in your city or town.

✳ Use local media as a resource. In some cities and towns, a local magazine will dedicate a single issue to rating the top doctors in the area (in the Big Apple, *New York* magazine does this every year and provides a resource on their Web site year round). You can also check Web sites, message boards, and neighborhood e-mail lists for local recommendations.

✳ Ask a lawyer. He or she might know someone who does medical malpractice defense. These people often know good doctors . . . or at least the ones to avoid!

✳ Depending on what type of medical coverage you have, you might need to pick from a list of doctors who are covered by your provider. Be sure to cross-check the above resources with this list.

Now that you've got a list of doctors in hand, it's time to do some research. Here are a few good resources to get you started:

✳ Google the doctor's name and see what you can find. Often a doctor will have a Web site that provides some basic biographical information.

✳ Visit your state medical licensing board Web site and search to verify that the doctor is currently licensed. If you can't find the right Web site, go to the American Medical Association for a link to your state's Medical Licensing Board: http://www.ama-assn.org/ama/pub/education-careers/ becoming-physician/medical-licensure/state-medical-boards.shtml, or check the American Board of Medical Specialties Web site (this service is free, but registration is required): https://www.abms.org/WC/login.aspx.

✳ Check out sites such as http://www.ratemds.com and http://www.healthgrades.com, where you can order a background check to see if the doctor has any malpractice claims against him or her and is in good standing with the state medical board.

While you're doing this research, think of yourself as a shmirshky private investigator at the center of a sexy espionage thriller. It's always the middle of a hot summer in those stories, so your hot flashes set the mood perfectly. Put on a big-brimmed hat and speak with a 1940s New York accent, and you'll be good to go. You see, looking for a gynecologist who specializes in PM&M can get pretty exciting!

shmirshky interview

After you gather doctor recommendations and research them thoroughly, make an appointment to meet the doctors and interview them. When you call, be sure to make it clear that this is an interview and not a checkup. I always offer to pay for the interview, but no one has ever charged me for his or her time. If someone does end up charging you, consider it money worth spending. Your well-being is worth the investment.

I know you might be thinking, "Research, recommendations, interviews—E, this is *way* too much work! I'm having a hard enough time getting dinner on the table, and the kitchen sink hasn't been fixed yet. There's just no time to do all of these tasks." But honestly, shmirshkies, this isn't as daunting as it sounds, especially considering all the time we spend on slightly less important matters.

Before I make a major change in the color or style of my hair, I usually make an appointment for a consultation. Yet before going through PM&M, I'd never had a consultation with a doctor. How ridiculous was that? My shmirshky is at least as important as my hair! It was time for a new process. It was time to think inside the box and put a high priority on my shmirshky needs. When you interview doctors, don't hold back. Ask *any and all* questions you have. I cannot stress this enough. It's your responsibility to be forthcoming with your doctor so he or she can be in the best position to help you.

It is helpful to take an *advocate* with you to your interview and other important doctor visits (and if you take your advocate out for lunch afterward, the trip can even be fun!). Your advocate can be a loved one, family member, or friend. Often when we do not feel well, we are not functioning at our full capacity and may not hear clearly or speak up. Your advocate can be your extra set of ears and eyes and can help brainstorm with you as you evaluate your choices later.

Before each interview, spend a few weeks using the Shmirshky Daily Symptoms Chart on page 168. It's helpful to fill out your chart at the *same time* each day. I keep mine by my bed, as I find I have more time at night than in the morning when I'm rushing to get to work. Don't worry, it only takes five minutes.

Charting will help you tell the doctor how you *feel*. Think about it: when you are in PM&M you can't remember yesterday, let alone what you felt like last week or last month. Filling out this chart every day will enable a doctor to better understand what you're going through, track your progress, and find a course of action that works for you. Happy Charting!

I learned about the shmirshky interview process through my own mistakes. I found my first doctor through a recommendation, but I didn't interview her. I did interview the next doctor, but I didn't spend any time preparing: I just listened and didn't ask many questions. In retrospect, I could have saved a tremendous amount of time and energy had I brought my symptoms, questions, and advocate along for the ride. I wish I had done my prep work back then, perhaps I would have hit my Shmirshky Jackpot much sooner (more on this in chapter 19, "Shmirshky Jackpot").

Later on in my journey, I smartened up and took a different approach. I'm going to tell you about that now, so keep in mind, I'm jumping ahead in the story. You erlicks might have a problem with me leapfrogging around like this, but what can I say, I'm a shmirshky and this is how we talk, so here I go!

With my lists of questions and symptoms, and with David in tow, I was off to find a doctor who would help us find me! David and I had two gynecologists to interview: one shmirshky and one erlick. (I would have interviewed a cat and a dog if I thought it would help.) The first interview was with the shmirshky. David and I were taken to an examination room. She seemed to want to interview my shmirshky first, so I figured, okay. I began rattling off my questions as she began perusing my shmirshky. Thank goodness this is not the custom for all interviews or they'd have to install stirrups on the set of *The View*. This doctor answered all my questions and was extremely open about her philosophy, all while examining my shmirshky—she was quite an impressive multitasker. She then announced that "everything looked good" and she would be happy to help me. (I wondered, if it didn't look so good down there, would she have told me her practice was full?)

In contrast, at our appointment with the erlick, we were guided into the doctor's private office. I quickly glanced around the room and was relieved to see just two comfy chairs opposite the doctor's desk, no stirrups in sight. This gynecologist was *very* interested in understanding how I felt, what I was going through, and what I had experienced along the way. David chimed in whenever he thought he could shed some light on my dark days. After much conversation, I whipped out my list of questions, but this doctor had already covered almost everything.

Afterward, over lunch, David and I rehashed the interviews, weighing the pros and cons of each doctor. Although tests indicate that I have near perfect hearing, David heard a lot that I missed during these interviews. He was listening intently and was clearly able to recall in detail many differences between these two doctors' philosophies and styles. *My* concentration, on the other hand, was impaired by my lack of sleep, by my highly emotional state, and by my nagging desire to rip off my annoying tight pants!

At each of your interviews, get a feel for how the doctor's office is run. Be sure to get answers to the following questions: How do you reach your doctor when you need to talk *during* office hours? Then ask what the doctor's *after*-hours protocol is. For example, who is on call: the doctor, another doctor, a nurse practitioner, or an answering machine? Remember the game called telephone we all played at sleepovers? You know, when everyone gets in a circle and the first person whispers something to the next gal, and then she is supposed to repeat exactly what she heard to the next gal, and so on and so on until the last person stands up and repeats what she heard? The original message is a scrambled mess by the time it gets to the end. Don't play the telephone game with your doctor's office. It could result in a misdiagnosis.

Next, get a feel for the doctor's approach to his or her specialty. What is the doctor's philosophy? Ask how he or she approaches preventative medicine and the treatment of symptoms. What tests and procedures does the doctor typically run? If there are controversial topics relating to the doctor's field, ask what his or her philosophy is about these subjects. When you're seeing a doctor for PM&M, ask about his or her philosophy on HRT* and other PM&M treatments (more on that fun stuff later in chapter 15, "To HRT or Not to HRT?"). You will get a good feel for the doctor's personality and approach to medicine by discussing these topics.

Also, ask the doctor how he or she feels about patients getting second opinions before making major medical decisions. A doctor is at his or her best and brightest when prioritizing the patient's well-being over personal ego. If your doctor has a problem with second opinions, think about switching to one who is not only comfortable with the practice but actually welcomes it.

Many shmirshkies avoid finding a good PM&M doctor as a last line of defense in the shmirshky "I'm fine" cover-up. After all, deciding to get help means accepting that you need help in the first place. Remember that we can't be "fine" all the time. If you're feeling overwhelmed, try allocating a specific time for each task. A phone call only takes a couple minutes. And in the end, taking these few extra research steps will actually be a

---

* HRT is short for hormone replacement therapy. The term HRT is pretty misleading, as no one fully "replaces" all of her hormones. Also called HT (hormone therapy or hormone treatment).

shortcut; the sooner you find the right PM&M specialist, the sooner you will feel better.

Break the cover-up cycle and be *honest* with your doctor. This sounds easy, but it's a bit challenging at first to be okay with not being "fine." Think of the doctor-patient relationship like you would a business partnership. Would you go into business with someone who doesn't listen to you and sincerely respect your opinion? You and your doctor are partners too. Both of you need to be able to communicate openly and freely. Your journey will be much easier if you have the right doctor on your team. Don't settle for less than you deserve!

shmirshky numbers

In addition to your yearly Pap smear* and mammogram,✝ you need to get some other tests to help you monitor your PM&M. These test results will help give you and your doctor an idea of where you are on your PM&M journey, but they are not definitive indicators. You have to pay close attention to your symptoms and to how you feel. It's not unheard of that a shmirshky's hormone numbers will appear normal while her PM&M symptoms are through the roof, because every shmirshky lives differently, at different hormone levels.

While the suggested test-result ranges I've included in this book can be helpful reference points, they should not be treated

---

* A Pap smear is an examination of cells scraped from the cervix. This sampling is then examined under a microscope by a pathologist to determine if any of the cells are cancerous or precancerous.

✝ A mammogram is an X-ray picture of the breasts. It is used to find tumors and to help tell the difference between noncancerous (benign) and cancerous (malignant) disease. You younger shmirshkies have the wonderful mammogram in your future! Be sure to take advantage of this test! It has caught many precancers and reduced the number of breast cancers in this country. If you can, find a place that has digital mammography, especially if you have dense (bumpy/lumpy) breasts.

as objective benchmarks. Be sure to bring your Shmirshky Daily Symptoms Chart and tell your doctor how you *feel*, because this helps determine what the test results mean for your body and how best to approach your particular situation. Discuss all the different options with your gynecologist and get the tests you need.

Below, I have listed the tests that I found helpful.* You can get most of these done with one blood draw. Always ask your doctor's office for a copy of your lab results and keep them in a notebook or folder. You may find you want to refer back to them later. There are lots of numbers here, but don't worry, no long division! Okay, here we go: ✢

✳ Bone density: Bone density is the measure of calcium and other minerals in your bones. The bone density test, also

---

* You might find that you don't need all of the tests I've listed or that you might need a few tests that aren't included in this list. More is not necessarily merrier when it comes to medical testing. It's more important to get accurate results for the tests you need. Always be conscious of false positives and ask your doctor about the accuracy of each test. It is so important to have a clear and accurate diagnosis before you begin any medical treatment.

✢ The suggested normal ranges listed here are for shmirshkies of all ages, except when otherwise specified. These ranges can change from year to year. There are always new advances and discoveries that result in new tests and different standards. There is no one concrete source for suggested number ranges. Different labs, hospitals, and doctors often have different suggested ranges. Be sure to consult with your doctor in order to home in on what range is best for you. All of these ranges and definitions are from the MedlinePlus Medical Encyclopedia, retrieved on October 9, 2010, from http://www.nlm.nih.gov/medlineplus/encyclopedia.html, unless otherwise noted here or in Additional Notes. For more detailed sources, see the corresponding Shmirshky Not-So-Fun Terms on page 136.

called a DEXA scan, is a great preventative test. It can determine whether you have osteoporosis[*] or even a risk of getting osteoporosis before you experience symptoms. When you go through PM&M, your estrogen[+] levels decline, which can lead to a rapid loss of bone density, so this is important for the PM&M shmirshky to check. The test measures the bone density (strength) of both the hip and spine. It only takes a few minutes and exposes you to very little radiation (technicians are not even required to wear a lead apron). Suggested range:

- *T-score*: greater than -1[✿]

✳ CA-125 (cancer antigen 125): This protein is best known as a blood marker for ovarian cancer. It may also be elevated with other malignant cancers, including those originating in the endometrium, fallopian tubes, lungs, breasts, and gastrointestinal tract. Suggested range:

- Less than 35 U/mL[*]

---

[*] Osteoporosis is a medical condition in which the bones become brittle, typically as a result of a hormonal deficiency or reduced calcium or vitamin D levels.
[+] Estrogen is the primary female hormone. Estrogen is responsible for the development and maintenance of female reproductive structures.
[✿] T-scores between -1 and -2.5 generally indicate the beginnings of bone loss, also known as osteopenia. T-scores at or below -2.5 typically indicate osteoporosis.
[*] The normal value range for CA-125 varies slightly among different laboratories. Unfortunately, this test can result in false positive results. Be sure to talk with your doctor about the pros and cons of this test.

✳ Cholesterol: A waxy substance produced by the body. It is needed to make hormones, skin cells, and digestive juices. Your cholesterol changes during PM&M. Too much cholesterol in your body can build up plaque in your arteries, which ultimately narrows the blood vessels and may cause a heart attack. You will need to fast for this test, so don't eat or drink for twelve hours beforehand. Suggested range:✳

- *Total cholesterol*: less than 200 mg/dL

- *HDL* (high-density lipoprotein, the "good" cholesterol): less than 50 mg/dL generally *increases* your risk of heart disease; greater than 60 mg/dL generally *helps protect against* heart disease.

- *LDL* (low-density lipoprotein, the "bad" cholesterol [too much LDL in the blood can clog your arteries]): less than 100 mg/dL

- *Triglycerides* (molecules of fatty acid): less than 150 mg/dL

- *Cholesterol/HDL* (the ratio of total cholesterol to HDL): less than 5:1 is desirable; 3.5:1 is optimum

✳ DHEAS: DHEA sulfate is a hormone that is easily converted into other hormones, including estrogen and testosterone. It

---

✳ The suggested ranges for Total cholesterol, HDL, LDL, and Triglycerides are from the American Heart Association. The suggested range for Cholesterol/HDL is from Lab Tests Online.

is the adrenal hormone that triggers puberty and is found in the highest concentration in the body. DHEAS is the sulfated (S) form of DHEA in the blood. DHEA levels increase and decrease throughout the day. DHEAS blood levels are steadier, and therefore more reliable. Suggested range:

- *Age 30–39*: 45–270 ug/dL

- *Age 40–49*: 32–240 ug/dL

- *Age 50–59*: 26–200 ug/dL

- *Age 60–69*: 13–130 ug/dL

- *Age 69 and older*: 17–90 ug/dL

✳ Estradiol: This is the main type of estrogen produced in the body. It is secreted by the ovaries. If you're still menstruating, be sure to have this blood test done during the first three days of your period. Suggested range:

- *Premenopausal*: 30–400 pg/mL

- *Postmenopausal*: 0–30 pg/mL

✳ Free and Total Testosterone: Free testosterone is the unbound, metabolically active testosterone. Total testosterone includes both the free and bound testosterone. In shmirshkies, the ovaries produce testosterone. This benefits shmirshkies by helping to maintain a healthy libido, strong bones, muscle mass, and mental stability. Suggested range:

- 30–95 ng/dL

✳ FSH (follicle stimulating hormone): A pituitary hormone that stimulates the growth of the ovum (the egg and surrounding cells that produce ovarian hormones). This is one of the measures that can indicate if you've entered M (although it's not a definitive determinant because your levels can fluctuate). If you're still menstruating, be sure to have this blood test done during the first three days of your period. Suggested range*:

- *Shmirshkies who are menstruating*: 1.7–21.5 mIU/mL

- *Postmenopausal shmirshkies*: 25.8–134.8 mIU/mL

✳ Progesterone: This is a hormone that stimulates the uterus and gets it ready for pregnancy.✢ Progesterone also regulates the monthly menstrual cycle. Low levels of progesterone can impact your mood and cause irritability, among other things. Results will vary depending on when the test is done. Suggested range:

- *Pre-ovulation*: less than 1 ng/mL

- *Mid-cycle*: 5–20 ng/mL

- *Postmenopausal*: less than 1 ng/mL

✱ The FSH suggested ranges are from LabCorp.com. Please make sure you check with your doctor and blood lab about the suggested ranges for your FSH test, as each lab tends to use a different range.

✢ You see, shmirshkies are always getting ready for something! Progesterone is like a hair and makeup person for your uterus: hustling to get you ready for the big event of pregnancy. In fact, the entire menstrual cycle is like getting ready for a ball that you rarely attend. You put on all your makeup, put your hair up all snazzy, and squeeze into a fancy dress. Then once you're ready to go, you decide, "Nah, let's just order in."

✳ Thyroid workup: This blood test usually includes checking your TSH (thyroid stimulating hormone). If there is an irregularity with your TSH, you may need to get your Total T3 and Free T4 checked as well. (*Free* means it won't be affected by your estrogen status, not free of charge!)✢ Remember that the symptoms for both PM&M and a thyroid disorder can be very similar. Suggested range:✖

- *Total T3*: 60–180 ng/dL

- *Free T4*: 0.89–1.76 ng/dL

- *TSH*: approximately 0.3–3.0 mIU/L for those with no symptoms of abnormal thyroid function. A much wider range of approximately 0.5 to 5.0 or even 6.0 mIU/L is being used by labs and doctors who are *not* following the latest recommendations by the American Association of Clinical Endocrinologists.✚

✢ T3 and T4 are thyroid hormones that get released into the bloodstream and control the body's metabolism.

✖ There is a great deal of discrepancy in the medical world regarding the suggested ranges for T3, T4, and TSH. There are many different institutions and doctors with varying opinions. The science seems to be ever evolving. My doctors recommended these ranges to me, but please do not take these ranges as gospel. Be sure to consult with your doctor to determine what range is most appropriate for your body.

✚ Depending on how you feel and your particular medical situation, your endocrinologist may want to keep your TSH lower than 3. Everyone is a little different. I happen to function best when mine is below 1.

✳ Vitamin D3 (Cholecalciferol): This vitamin, named after my husband's first initial, helps to maintain normal blood levels of calcium and phosphorus, and helps keep your bones nice and strong. Suggested range:✳

- 40–100 ng/mL

Most of these tests are simple blood tests, which is actually a nice break from having lots of things shoved in and out of our shmirshky at the gynecologist. When we go to the gyno for a Pap smear, we're told to get undressed, put on a gown, and put our heels in the stirrups. When I hear *gown*, I start looking for something beaded and satin, but instead I get a paper towel jacket and a giant paper towel tablecloth to drape over my legs. During the exam, I never have a clue what's going on down there. Do you? My gynecologist always tells me, "Just relax." Yeah, I'll relax when you stop sticking giant Q-tips up my shmirshky. I can't wait to grab that huge paper towel, mop up all the gel they shoved inside me, and get the hell out of there. Doesn't this process sound a bit archaic? At least upgrade the paper towel to two-ply or quilted. I hope the Brawny Man doesn't walk in on me while I'm all saddled up!

✳ The suggested range for Vitamin D3 is from the American Academy of Orthopedic Surgeons.

to hrt or not to hrt?

Once your test results come in, be sure to make an appointment to meet with your doctor in person to discuss your numbers. Bring your advocate with you on this visit as well. I brought my husband so that he too would become more aware and involved in what I was going through. After all, we were going through it together. The more I included David in my journey, the more knowledgeable, helpful, and supportive he became. Plus, let's face it, by this point I was a total bitchface half the time. David pretty much jumped at any opportunity to get back the wife he knew and loved.

Remember that the results of your lab work are only half of the conversation. At this appointment you need to be sure to bring your Shmirshky Daily Symptoms Chart and communicate honestly and openly about how you're feeling. Ask your advocate to help encourage this during your appointment. Make notes before your appointment of all the things you want to talk about. Share this list with your advocate. The more clearly your doctor understands how you're feeling and functioning, the more he or she will be able to help determine the correct course of action for you.

Don't feel rushed. Doctors are often on a tight schedule and they like to move quickly, but don't let that frazzle you or steer you off course. Set the pace of your appointment so that you and your advocate can address all your questions and concerns.

The big question at this stage is whether to HRT * or not to HRT. In order to answer this question, we need to have a quick crash course on HRT. Basically, the way it works is that when you go through PM&M, your body begins to produce different amounts (usually smaller) of estrogen, progesterone, and/or testosterone hormones. These fluctuations often result in the symptoms that many PM&M shmirshkies experience. HRT is intended to supplement or moderate these hormone fluctuations and ultimately provide an umbrella for a shmirshky caught in a PM&M storm.

Not all HRT options are created equal. The first distinction you will want to make is whether an HRT supplement is bio-identical or not (see Hormone Therapy Brands on page 156). A bioidentical hormone is identical to the hormone produced in your body. It may not have originated in your body, but it has the same chemical structure and even goes by the same name. Most important, it has the same biological function.✢

On the other hand, there are HRT options available that are NOT identical to the hormones in your body. They might

---

* Hormone replacement therapy; also called HT (hormone therapy or hormone treatment).
✢ The most common bioidentical hormones prescribed for PM&M shmirshkies are estradiol, estrone, estriol, progesterone, and testosterone.

be similar, they might even have a similar name, but they are not exactly the same as the hormones produced in your body.[*]

The other important characteristic to understand is whether or not the HRT option is natural and/or synthetic. I say "and/or" here because the natural and synthetic labels are NOT mutually exclusive. Here's how that works. Technically speaking, if a hormone is called *natural*, that means it is originally derived from a plant or animal source. A hormone is considered *synthetic* if the chemical structure was altered in a laboratory. Sometimes hormones are extracted from yams and then chemically altered. In this instance, the hormone is both natural and synthetic.[+]

If you're given a prescription for HRT and want to know what you're getting, try asking the following questions:

- Is this HRT option bioidentical? Or, in other words: Is this HRT option chemically identical to the hormone I produce in my body?

- Was this HRT chemically altered in a lab? (If the answer is yes, then the HRT option is a synthetic hormone.)

---

[*] Don't be fooled by a hormone with two names. Even if one of those names is the name of your body's hormone, the presence of another name should tip you off that you are NOT dealing with a bioidentical hormone. For example, estradiol is bioidentical, but ethinyl estradiol is NOT.

[+] Defining the terms *natural hormone* and *synthetic hormone* can be complicated and confusing. Many different Web sites, books, and journals use conflicting definitions for these terms. For the purposes of this book, I am using very simple and technical definitions as recommended by my doctors. Please note that some experts and resources might use different definitions for these terms, but I am choosing to define them in a way that I believe is the most technically accurate, the least confusing, and the most helpful.

✳ Did this hormone originate in a plant or animal? (If yes, then that hormone is technically considered natural.)

If the answer to all three questions is yes, then you have a plant- or animal-derived hormone that was chemically altered to become identical to a hormone found in your body—which means it is natural, synthetic, and bioidentical. I know it's confusing, because natural and synthetic seem like opposites, but with regard to HRT, they are actually referring to two different distinctions. Whoever came up with these terms needs a talking to.✳

These distinctions are important, because just as your body reacts differently to a tablet of Advil than it does to a tablet of Aleve, different hormone therapy options have different potentially positive and negative results. When you take bioidentical hormone therapy, your body may react the same way it would if it produced the hormone itself, because, chemically speaking, it is the same as the hormone your body actually does produce. When you take hormone therapy that is not bioidentical, your body may react differently.✥ Learn about how your medication options might affect your body before you decide with your doctor on a particular course of treatment.

✳ If this doesn't make total sense the first time around, don't feel bad. It took me years to fully understand what all this stuff means. Try reading the last few paragraphs again, this time slower and without grinding your teeth! If you're still confused, just go to shmirshky.com or e-mail me at e@shmirshky.com and I'll walk you through it!

✥ Keep in mind that there are many schools of thought on this, and it is up to you to educate yourself and draw your own conclusions about what is best for your body.

Now that you've gotten a handle on your HRT lingo, you need to learn about the WHI (Women's Health Initiative)* and the studies it conducted. There are many different viable interpretations of these studies, so it is best that you go online to the Women's Health Initiative at www.nhlbi.nih.gov/whi and read about the studies for yourself. To further research what some experts think of the validity of these tests and their findings, do a Web search for "WHI pros and cons." You can read for hours. Let me caution you right now, this is not fun reading! Many nights, I could have used some toothpicks to prop my eyelids open because the material is so technical and dry.

Here is what I learned: The FDA+ announced its statement on the WHI studies in 2002, which scared every PM&M shmirshky half to death. The agency reported that HRT increases a shmirshky's risk of breast cancer and heart disease. It was all over the newspapers and news shows. So many shmirshkies went off their HRT cold turkey! OMG! That's like stopping a roller coaster on a dime in the middle of the ride. You're left hanging upside down, lucky if you don't fall right out of your seat!

I am not a scientist or a doctor, but let me tell you a few of the problems that I have with these studies. Some of the shmirshkies in these studies had heart disease, were obese,

---

✷ The Women's Health Initiative was created by the National Heart, Lung, and Blood Institute, a division of the National Institutes of Health under the U.S. Department of Health and Human Services. The WHI conducted a series of clinical trials and observational studies on postmenopausal shmirshkies.

+ The Food and Drug Administration is a federal agency that oversees the safety regulations of most types of food, supplements, drugs, vaccines, and medical products.

and had elevated cholesterol levels requiring medication. All of the shmirshkies who were studied were in Post-M and were given the same amount of HRT. This was not clear to many PM shmirshkies, who thought the studies applied directly to them. Do you think a shmirshky who is seventy-nine years old should be treated with the same dose of HRT as a shmirshky who is fifty? No, as you get older, you typically require less HRT, and shmirshkies in PM require very different treatments than shmirshkies in M and Post-M.

It is also important to note what kind of HRT was used in the studies. Up until 2002, most shmirshkies on HRT were taking Provera or Premarin (a mixture of estrogens obtained from the urine of pregnant horses).* Many shmirshkies were on Prempro (which is a combination of Provera and Premarin). The WHI studies were solely focused on these forms of HRT, none of which are bioidentical.

Why didn't they also study healthy, younger shmirshkies while they were in the beginning stages of PM&M and see how they fared with various kinds of HRT? I think we should all demand more studies on HRT and PM&M. We need more hormone specialists, please! We need to keep our scientists studying and researching this. With all the brains in this country, is this the best we can do for shmirshkies? I think NOT!

It is so important to think inside the box and educate yourself on the issues. Be sure to read more about bioidentical hormones and, once again, brace yourself for some new vocab

---

* Whooaaaaa, horsie! Horses are such huge animals. I already feel so big; I don't need any help in that department. Horses are beautiful, don't get me wrong, but couldn't we get urine from something petite and lithe . . . like a *Cover Girl* model?

words, not-so-fun terms like progesterone,⁑ estradiol,× estrone,+ and estriol.❃ You'll also need to familiarize yourself with the various forms that HRT comes in. You won't believe how many options there are! (Check out the Hormone Therapy Menu on page 154.) You can wear a patch. These patches are like putting medicine on a piece of Scotch tape. Seriously, that is what it looks like. Then you have the cream version. You can use the cream topically (on your skin) or shoot it right into your shmirshky (this was news to me!). Then there are pills. You can put them under your tongue and let them dissolve, swallow them, or shoot those babies right into your shmirshky too. Then there is the ring. No, I'm not referring to a diamond one; this one does not go on your finger. Guess where it goes? Yep, in the shmirshky. There are also pellets they can shoot right under your skin. Don't forget the sprays, but these, thank goodness, you spray on your skin (not on your hair!).

As I was researching, I started to visualize my carry-on bag at the airport. My allowable toiletry Baggie was already bulging with all the face creams I had squeezed into tiny three-ounce bottles. I definitely could not risk putting my shmirshky creams in the same bag as all of those face creams—what if I got them

---

⁑ Progesterone gets the uterus ready for pregnancy and the breasts ready for milk production. After ovulation, progesterone helps make the uterus ready for implantation of a fertilized egg. Remember, shmirshkies are always getting ready for something! When your ovaries stop producing progesterone and estrogen, you're in M, and you don't have to get ready for the pregnancy party that you usually don't end up going to each month.

× Estradiol is the most important form of estrogen produced in the body.

+ Estrone is one of the three most common types of estrogen secreted by the ovaries.

❃ Estriol is the weakest of the three main types of estrogen.

mixed up? Homeland Security needs to get right on this! We may need a special line at airport security for PM&M shmirshkies.

So many choices! I was overwhelmed!

My mind immediately wandered to my favorite shoe store. I love buying shoes. (FYI, your shoe size is the only size that doesn't seem to change with PM&M.) I can walk around the biggest shoe department and have no problem whatsoever picking out one pair that I love. Too bad they can't administer HRT through a pair of heels.

I began talking to every shmirshky I knew. No matter where I was—in a grocery store, at the cleaners, in a car wash, or at a dinner party—I would bring up the topic. I had no time to be wishy-washy, so I was very direct, asking every shmirshky young and old, "Do you take HRT?" Based on the reactions I got, you would have thought I was talking about a nasty drug habit! It seemed no one wanted to admit that they use or used HRT. It was *taboo*. I think the fallout over the WHI* study made a lot of shmirshkies think that being on HRT was wrong, so they sort of went into hiding (back under the bush). But I didn't give up.

——————————— shmirshky party alert!

Y Gloria, now seventy-plus years old, was on Premarin and Provera for years for her PM&M symptoms (sleep disturbances and night sweats). Like so many

---

* Women's Health Initiative.

shmirshkies, when the WHI study came out, Gloria abruptly stopped taking hormone therapy. Unfortunately, her symptoms reappeared, so she tried several bioidentical options for a couple years, but her breasts became so tender (a symptom that is often caused by estrogen dominance✢) that she could no longer sleep on her stomach. The public stir about hormone therapy risks, coupled with her nagging breast tenderness, led Gloria to discontinue her HRT altogether.

Now here is Gloria's *recurring* evening forecast: sleepless with mild to heavy precipitation (those beloved night sweats are back). I feel so bad that Gloria is still suffering. I picture myself at age seventy-three, still sleepless and dripping. Yikes, thank goodness shmirshkies don't get mildew!

Y In contrast, Patty's response to my "Do you take HRT?" survey was wholeheartedly positive. "HRT is on my list of very positive experiences," she said. Patty explained that she always had the world's best memory, until, suddenly, during PM&M, it vanished. She was on the verge of tears all of the time and was no longer joyful or a joy to live with. I asked her husband, Mark, what it was like to live with Patty before she

---

✢ Estrogen dominance refers to the situation in which there is too much estrogen relative to the amount of progesterone in a woman's body. When estrogen dominates, there is a greater risk of heavy menstrual bleeding and other symptoms.

went on HRT. He said it was "like a roller coaster ride," fun when you're five, not so much when you're fifty. Once Patty began bioidentical creams, though, her life turned around. She describes it as an "And then there was light!" moment. She became a whole new person— no more emotional roller coaster rides or night sweats. She slept better, became less forgetful, more focused, more patient, and more present. After HRT, if she found herself in a bad mood, her daughter and son would jokingly ask, "Mom, did you use your cream today?"

My friend Mindy is a whole other story. When she comes into town every August for a week, we like to hit the beach and catch up on shmirshky news. The young, frolicking, bikini-clad shmirshkies run around the beach while Mindy and I sit smothered in SPF 60 under a huge oversized umbrella with our towels draped over our chalky white legs. As it turns out, I envy Mindy's PM&M experience almost as much as I envy how the younger shmirshkies' butts stay politely tucked into their bikini bottoms.

Mindy basically experienced "PM&M light" and never felt the need to take HRT. Her first symptom began at fifty-one when her periods became irregular and then completely stopped for one full year. She had one more "encore" period and then it was gone forever. The show was over. Mindy never had a sleepless night, a dry shmirshky, or memory loss, but she did have some problems with her internal thermometer. Sometimes her husband would find her sitting on the sofa stripped of her top and bra, but before he had a chance to get excited, she would have herself wrapped in a blanket because she was cold. Lucky for Mindy, her temperature fluctuations only lasted for about six months and never resulted in a drop of sweat. She told me, "At fifty-three I became a bitch. Of course, I blamed it on menopause, because with no period, you can't blame it on PMS anymore!" Her PM&M symptoms faded away by age fifty-four, leaving Mindy all out of excuses!

Ultimately every shmirshky has to make her own determination about what course of action is best for her body. For Gloria, it's being HRT free, and for Patty and her family, it's an HRT shrine next to the fireplace. For Mindy, she has to find a new excuse when she's being a bitchface!

I was hoping one of my friends would just tell me what to do, but that universal answer didn't exist. Everyone's case was so different and required different solutions. So how was I going to decide? If I were to use HRT, what other side effects would I have? Would I gain more weight? Oh, dear! Would I have more or less risk of cancer? Would HRT prevent osteoporosis or make me more susceptible to broken bones? I kept reading and educating myself so that I could make the healthiest choices. I can't stress enough the importance of research—take responsibility for your body and arm yourself with knowledge. If you decide not to HRT, acupuncture (see chapter 22, "No Needles in My Shmirshky") can be a tremendous help. Some shmirshkies combine HRT and acupuncture with great success.

Ultimately, you and your doctor will need to decide what is right for you. Depending on your medical history, your options may be very different. A good starting point is to simply think inside the box. Ask yourself, on a scale of 1 to 10: How am I functioning? How is my life? Some shmirshkies are so used to being less than functioning that they find themselves accepting a 2 as normal. You don't have to settle. Once you know your challenges, you can begin to find the right solutions. Whatever you do, don't give up trying to be as close to 10 as possible. You deserve it!

shmirshky support

I used to have a consistently even personality, but during my PM&M storm, David and I never knew which me we were going to wake up to. Sometimes I thought I was going to have a good day, but more often than not the storm came in and I felt out of control. No way, no how could I simply talk myself down from this. I was desperate to get some sleep, have a clear head again, and stop being the primo HS.*

Wherever I went, my mind was on PM&M. One day I was in New York taking the subway uptown during rush hour. The subway was packed. Everyone else seemed to be daydreaming or thinking about work and the challenges of their day. Not me. I gazed at all the shmirshkies on the subway and had the strongest desire to ask them about their PM&M. I sat there wondering if they were in PM, or if they had finished M. I guessed that some of the grumpy shmirshkies whose pants were so tight that their shmirshky was going to break in two (you know what I'm talking about) were smack in the middle of it.

My ears perked up whenever I heard someone on the news

---

* Hot shmirshky!

or a talk show speaking about HRT or PM&M. I listened to everything I could (thank you, DVR and TiVo!). I couldn't help but notice that many celebrity talk show hosts were going through PM&M right before my eyes. I saw them struggling, heard them explain that they turned the air conditioning way up as their internal thermostats went completely askew. Of course, all the non-PM&M hosts were freezing. This reminded me of David trying to sleep in our bedroom with the air conditioning on in the dead of winter. Poor guy.

Ultimately, the HRT decision was mine to make. Along with my gynecologist at the time, I decided that it would be good for me to begin HRT. I was nervous at first, but the one constant comfort for me was the support of the Sisterhood. We need to be there for each other. The more I opened up to my friends and loved ones, the more comforted I became. Their support helped me to embrace my PM&M. I stopped being in such a hurry to fix me and became calmer and more accepting of where and who I was. I was learning how to be okay with not being "fine," and I felt a little better.

Talking with other shmirshkies who have gone through PM&M is as important as studying the most current research and conferencing with your doctor. There are all kinds of ways to get this shmirshky support. It is easy to take your morning exercise crew, book club, birthday lunch bunch, cooking club, carpool group, play group, investment club, or cocktail circle and turn it into a shmirshky support group just by talking, asking, and sharing your PM&M experience. If you aren't in any kind of club or group, start your own—host a Shmirshky Party!

Use the Internet to reach out to the shmirshky diaspora.

Most shmirshkies' Web sites have blogs, Webcasts, and forums where you can type in what you're going through and get support and advice from other shmirshkies. Visit shmirshky.com and connect to other PM&M shmirshkies around the world. PM&M shmirshkies are everywhere, and we need each other, so don't be afraid to reach out for help.

period or no period?

After months on an HRT regimen, my period went from arriving irregularly to not coming at all. I thought I had graduated from PM to M. It had been thirty-nine years since my period first showed up. Can you believe that? I'd been dealing with that damn period for thirty-nine years! You'd think I would have been relieved when my period stopped, but it was oddly sad to me. I found myself going through the grieving process. I think it was more the realization that I was getting older rather than feeling sad about not having a period. That being said, I was certainly thrilled to dispose of all my period paraphernalia. I was especially joyous to get rid of my tampons and pads with wings; they, of course, flew right out of the box. Too bad there was no party or presents to go along with my period's departure, though I was thinking about putting a graduation cap on my shmirshky.

I was convinced the period and I were done until one Sunday afternoon at a summer BBQ at my house with twenty-two friends. I was wearing this wonderful white sundress and felt relaxed and carefree, until I stood up to get someone another drink and saw the horror on my guests' faces. There I was with my period soaked through my dress *and* the sofa I was sitting on. My face all of a sudden matched my dress. Where are those pads with wings when you need them, flying to the rescue? I left the party and ran to my room, showered, and put my white dress in a sink full of stain remover. The stains disappeared before my eyes. Was there a way to drink that stuff and make my period disappear?

The funny thing was, after this period I felt really good. Go figure. Still, I wanted so desperately to skip past all this PM&M madness and go right to the big finale when the heroine is dancing and smiling and living happily ever after in a beautiful dress with a chorus of singers carrying her off into the sunset. I was so exasperated with this whole process. I kept thinking that I would like to exchange my shmirshky for an erlick (good thing my mom kept the receipt in her purse!).

erlicks are people too

I know they say the grass is always greener on the other side, but it just seemed to me that erlicks have it easy. All they have to do is decide if their erlicks should dangle to the left or to the right. I could do that, no problem. I've been wearing earrings and necklaces all my life, and they all dangle. How hard could this be?

From the moment erlicks are born, someone is caring for their erlick. Our son, Jack, found his when he was a baby, and after that, he never wanted to let it go. When he was a toddler, he even answered the door holding it. My mom was appalled. I explained to her that it was natural and we shouldn't mention it, as that would bring attention to it. I thought he would outgrow it. But do erlicks ever outgrow it? Not really. Someone (if not themselves) is always holding the erlick.

In all seriousness, I know you erlicks have your share of health issues as well. There is, in fact, such a thing as male menopause, although that term is a bit flimsy, since erlicks don't menstruate. While a shmirshky's PM&M is all about the slowdown and eventual shutdown of her reproductive system, erlicks can typically produce sperm well into their eighties (I think there is a story about Moses making use of this feature). Still, some erlicks do experience hormone fluctuations that may cause symptoms similar to PM&M, like fatigue, depression, physical weakness, and a lower libido.

Menopause-like symptoms in erlicks are not to be ignored or laughed off—they may be the result of dropping testosterone levels or a thyroid condition. If you're an erlick who is struggling, don't suffer in silence. Reach out to your internist, endocrinologist, and the people you love to get the help you need.

I must admit, when I first heard about male menopause, it reminded me of the first time I was pregnant, when I started to get these ravenous cravings for strange food combinations. That was probably my favorite part of being pregnant—I ate everything in sight! Being the ever-supportive husband that he was, it didn't take long before David started to get cravings of his own. He gained ten pounds during both of my pregnancies. I guess he just really wanted to get in on the experience (or the pickles and ice cream).

With David's sympathy cravings in full swing, I was thrilled to have an eating partner in crime. Years later, his hormones began to fluctuate around the same time as my PM&M. Of course, menopause isn't contagious, it was just a coincidence of age, but the thought of two hormonally imbalanced people living side by side was downright frightening.＊

It began with the thyroid for David, just like me. All of a sudden, he was lethargic. I thought, well, maybe he's just so

---

＊ Lesbian shmirshkies know all about this. Double the shmirshkies, double the PM&M!

exhausted from dealing with me, it's finally catching up to him! In addition to being tired, he was getting forgetful and his libido was dropping. We talked about how he was feeling and he decided to go to the doctor. David got his thyroid and hormone levels checked and found out that he had a minor thyroid condition *and* his testosterone levels were taking a nosedive. What a great husband—if it wasn't pickles and ice cream, it was testosterone and synthroid.✛

While you're at it, don't forget to check the rearview mirror. Shmirshkies and erlicks have the same next-door neighbor, which we all have to get checked out with a colonoscopy,✖ usually when we hit our fifties. Don't forget to do this; it's very important for everyone. In addition to prostate cancer and all the other health issues erlicks have, you really do go through PM&M along with us shmirshkies. At least there isn't an "erlickogram," where you have to put your balls between two flat, cold metal slabs to be smashed together as tightly as possible while you hold your breath!

✛ Synthroid is one of the medications commonly used to treat hypothyroidism.
✖ A colonoscopy is an examination of the large colon and part of the small bowel with a curious little camera they stick up shmirshky and erlick's next-door neighbor. Is this more fun than a Pap smear? Have one of each and then decide.

shmirshky jackpot

My period was like gum on a shoe, and I still was not function-ing well. I wasn't sleeping, my night sweats persisted, and my breasts were growing like water balloons. My boobs got so big that one afternoon, while sitting in a boardroom meeting with four other people, a button actually popped right off my blouse and onto the table! Everyone pretended they didn't see it, which I suppose is the polite thing to do when a shmirshky's bra is suddenly exposed during a business meeting. If I had known I was going to give a show that day, I would have worn a much sexier bra. I was mortified! Luckily, I was wearing a blazer to cover up my big hips, so I was able to use the blazer to conceal the gaping hole in my blouse.

Needless to say, I started to question my HRT regimen. It seemed that my gynecologist at the time had a "one-size-fits-all" way of handling patients. I kept thinking that there must be a better way of determining how to home in on my specific needs so that I would function at a more optimum level. I was intent on finding a new doctor.

I had to go through *several* gynecologists and different courses of action until I eventually hit the jackpot. I was at a dinner party with a very revered and wonderful retired gynecologist. We were loading the dishwasher, and all of a sudden I just unloaded all my PM&M challenges. As tears streamed down my face, frustration and sadness poured out of me. Our host was so sweet, comforting, and reassuring. He told me that I did not have to feel this way. He assured me that he had a gynecologist for me to go to, one who understood that there isn't a one-size-fits-all answer for every shmirshky. This doctor had been studying PM&M for quite some time and would find the answers that were right for me.

As soon as I got home, I went right to my computer and began reading all I could about this referral. In addition, the next morning I called other shmirshkies to see if any of them had heard of this doctor. Then I made an appointment for David and me to interview him. I was anxious for this appointment and hopeful that there were better days ahead for me.

I LOVE LOVE LOVE this doctor! He was truly a godsend. He gathered detailed information about all of my symptoms in a manner and depth that no other doctor had ever done. By doing this he was able to zero in on my personal needs; he treated me in a very specific and conservative fashion. At long last, I had a partner helping with my decisions. I had finally hit my shmirshky jackpot!

shmirshky redecorated

Shmirshkies love to redecorate. We change our hair color at the drop of a hat, the length of our dresses, the color of our walls, and the layout of our living rooms. We love to remodel things. Often if we don't like something, we just get rid of it.

Let me stop right here and say that if you think that all is solved if you redecorate the shmirshky by having a hysterectomy,* you are in for a rude awakening. If you're told by your doctor to have a hysterectomy, *please, please, please* be sure to get a couple of opinions before you book the surgery. Remember, reaching out is IN; suffering in silence is OUT.

─────────── shmirshky party alert!

 My friend Joan found out she was estrogen dominant✢ (see chapter 15, "To HRT or Not to HRT?"),

---

* A hysterectomy is an operation in which the uterus is removed.
✢ Estrogen dominance occurs when there's too much estrogen relative to progesterone in a shmirshky's body. Heavy bleeding and sometimes even cancer can result from this.

and her gynecologist immediately told her that she needed to have a hysterectomy. Instead of rushing into surgery, she got a second opinion and ultimately decided against surgery.

Y Gloria's experience was very similar, although it happened thirty years earlier. Gloria was estrogen dominant as well, and her doctor told her, "If you were my wife, your uterus would be in a jar." That's pretty harsh language. I wonder how he would react if someone told him, "If you were my husband, your testicles would be in the trash." Gloria canned the doctor and the surgery. Remember, second opinions are always a good idea.

_____

Many shmirshkies do not do this; they just get one opinion. Listen carefully: when you have a hysterectomy *and* your ovaries are removed, your body goes immediately into M. As you can imagine, this can be quite a shocker to both your body and your soul! Other potential side effects of a hysterectomy may include incontinence* and pain during sex. It's important to be sure you *really* need to do this. Discuss your options and the potential side effects with your doctor. I read a wonderful article in *More*

_____

* Incontinence refers to the loss of bladder control. For shmirshkies, this can mean anything from mild drips to full-on floods.

Magazine's December 2008/January 2009 issue called "The Endangered Uterus" by Peg Rosen (love the title!). Take a look at
this before you redecorate.

——————— shmirshky party alert!

Erin had a complete hysterectomy in 1991. "I did
not think this surgery was going to be so devastating to my way of life," she says. Erin is now sixty-
three and recently had to have a second surgery—for
incontinence. She describes the surgery as "The kind
most women apparently do not like to talk about."
Incontinence is not entirely uncommon for shmirshkies who have had their uterus removed, because the
uterus holds up other organs in a shmirshky's body.
As Beth Battaglino Cahill puts it in "The Endangered
Uterus" article, "Removing [the uterus] is like pulling
out the cork from an upside-down wine bottle. Unless the woman has strong muscles, her bladder or her
bowels can descend into her vagina." I admire Erin
for sharing her experience. It's a good reminder that
surgery can sometimes cause as many problems as it
solves.

———————————————————————

Not all shmirshkies experience the devastating side effect
that Erin did. After several consultations, Darby and Monica

each found that they needed to have a hysterectomy. Their doctors spent time preparing them for the post-surgical hormonal responses. Together with their doctors they developed a customized plan for post-surgery shmirshky health.

─────────────── shmirshky party alert!

Darby was thirty-nine years old, married for two years, and was "Deliriously happy with a perfect sex life." She told me, "I had a period that came every twenty-eight days like clockwork, blessedly light flow, no cramps, bloating, or other problems. Then suddenly it all changed and I began having erratic periods, heavy flow with spotting in between, insomnia, mood swings, and cramps." It turned out that Darby had endometriosis* and her ovaries were in cell change.✝ "My doctor prepared me for surgically induced menopause," she said. "I was put on HRT immediately after surgery. I have been completely free of menopausal miseries ever since, and have the bonus of not having to worry about contracting ovarian, uterine, or cervical cancer."

---

* Endometriosis occurs when tissues that behave just like the cells that line a shmirshky's uterus grow in other areas of the body (usually in the pelvic area, outside the uterus, on the ovaries, bowel, rectum, or bladder).
✝ In Darby's case, her cells were behaving abnormally and could possibly have turned cancerous. Unfortunately, when cells behave badly, you can't just put them in "time out"; sometimes they need to be removed all together.

Monica was in her late fifties when she redecorated. Her doctor had a tremendous amount of problems balancing her HRT. As she explained, "I was turning into a crazy person—bleeding and possessed. I had a hysterectomy in my late fifties (eight years ago). It was done laparoscopically. I am not a bit disfigured by it, and in fact, I have a perfect menopausal body. This surgery saved my life and my marriage."

It's important to be cautious like Joan and Gloria, but if you find, after getting multiple opinions like Darby and Monica, that a hysterectomy is the *only* solution for you, then be sure to find a doctor who will take the time to tell you what you'll be experiencing and help you understand your options. Peg Rosen's article also gives you a list of all the different styles you can choose from. You can't pick from traditional, contemporary, or California classic, but you have choices. Read about them!

sex in the desert

I was born in Flint, Michigan, but when I was five we moved to Tucson, Arizona. I loved the desert. I always thought it was beautiful. What does this have to do with PM&M, you ask? When you're in PM&M, before you realize it, you may find that you're lost in a sex slump. Your shmirshky switches from naked and frolicking on a tropical island to being spiteful and stranded in the Mojave Desert. You find yourself doing anything you can to avoid going to bed. Let me just stop here and say that there were no crumbs in my kitchen drawers, nor a hair floating anywhere in my bathroom. My kitchen sink sparkled, and every e-mail anyone ever wrote me suddenly required an immediate response before I could even consider going to bed. Are you getting my drift? Our wonderful afternoon delights turned into trips to get ice cream. Basically our sex life took an immediate nosedive . . . only not into shmirshky land!

Part of this slump was caused by my extremely dry shmirshky. Sex hurt! Those two words should not be back to back. Let's face it; you need an ocean to surf! These changes seemed to creep up on me. Of course, I was trying to be "fine."

I tried subtly sneaking in questions to my fellow shmirshkies about this problem. Everyone danced around it until I got the courage to just come right out with it and ask, "Did your sex life change? Was your shmirshky dry?" Don't misunderstand me, the shmirshky doesn't suddenly look like a prune—it's the inside that feels like it has been dehydrated!

I found out that almost every PM&M shmirshky I talked to had experienced some time in the desert, and every one of us was embarrassed to talk with our doctors about this issue. Shmirshkies, let's not take the orgasm out of our lives! No need to do that!

You may find that these symptoms hit you later in your PM&M path. When this happens, pick up the phone, call your doctor, and ask to have your free/total testosterone and estrogen checked. You may have had them checked three months ago and they were normal, but with these symptoms, it is possible that they're not at a functional level anymore. Low testosterone contributes to a lack of sex drive. Low estrogen contributes to vaginal dryness. Low is not fun! There *is* help for this. Take a page out of my book and don't be afraid to be open and speak freely with your doctor. My new doctor fixed this problem in no time by adjusting my HRT. Share your sexual challenges with your partner as well. This open communication is so much healthier and might even make dealing with the challenge a little less stressful.

With a little lube and/or HRT, you can be back frolicking on the beach in no time! Now you can give those flannel pajamas you've been sleeping in a few nights off. You know what I'm referring to, the pj's that say "closed for business" to your partner. Find some fun new things to sleep in! "The change" doesn't have to be such a downer . . . instead, change it up!

CHAPTER TWENTY-TWO

no needles in my shmirshky

I am excited to report that I eventually did find some truly magic hands! I learned from my shmirshky recon that some shmirshkies found great relief from hot flashes and other PM&M symptoms by receiving acupuncture.*

———————— shmirshky party alert!

I passed that information on to my friend Cory, who was really struggling with hot flashes. She didn't want to go on HRT, so she tried acupuncture. I loved hearing how successful this was for Cory. Are you sitting down? After four appointments she was freed from her random drench sessions! Cory still visits every once in a while as part of her health regimen or perhaps just to hug the acupuncturist for turning off her leaking faucet. Recently, Cory notched up her

---

* Acupuncture is a practice developed in China of inserting fine needles through the skin at specific points to cure disease or relieve pain.

work-out routine by adding more cardio. The combination of acupuncture and aerobic exercise (*intentional* perspiration can be so wonderful) helped alleviate her mood swings as well. Acupuncture, like any medical treatment, is meant to be just one part of an overall healthy lifestyle. Go, Cory!

Y Janice is another shmirshky who managed her PM&M symptoms with acupuncture. Janice went to a school of acupuncture once a week (sometimes twice a week at first). Her dominant PM&M symptoms were heart palpitations and anxiety. There were nights when Janice would lie in bed with her heart pounding so hard that she thought she was about to have a heart attack. Can you imagine how scary that was? Janice decided to give acupuncture a whirl, and she ended up taking a Chinese herbal cocktail (I prefer vodka, personally) along with her acupuncture treatments. She said that while the acupuncture didn't totally relieve her symptoms, it helped significantly. Janice, like Cory, now continues to visit her acupuncturist as part of her general health routine.

Of course, you want to be sure that whomever you go to has a national and state license, and is well trained. Be sure to do your research.* Some acupuncturists want to give you all kinds of herbs along with your treatment; remember that these are medicines too.

While my HRT was starting to make an impact, I wanted to try acupuncture for myself. I should have asked Cory or Janice where they put the needles, because my palms were wet and beads of sweat were racing down my face as I walked toward the acupuncturist's office. I subtly patted the sweat off my forehead as I looked down to see if my shmirshky was sweating. It had been a while since that had happened, but my shmirshky was really scared.

I didn't want anyone to think I was having a minor panic attack, but let's be honest, it was a cool spring day and I looked like I had just walked out of a sauna. I wasn't fooling anyone. I thought my shmirshky was about to become a pincushion.

Once I entered the office lobby, the whole feeling of the space immediately calmed me. I filled out pages and pages of forms about my health, medications, vitamins, etc., and then the acupuncturist and I discussed my situation in great depth. I was taken with the amount of time that she spent with me and the detail of her questions. I gave her a copy of my most recent hormone, TSH, and cholesterol lab work. Next we went into a small room that looked similar to a massage room. There was a bed covered in sheets. I was told to get undressed (but keep my underwear on) and slip under the sheets. "Keep my

---

* You can find information on each state's licensing board at http://www .acupuncture.com/statelaws/statelaw.htm.

underwear on?" I thought. "No needles in my shmirshky!" I tried to keep my elation under wraps, but inside I was having a private shmirshky party.

The acupuncturist was very gentle. It was so interesting to me that there wasn't even one needle near my shmirshky. Quite honestly, it all went so smoothly that I'm not sure where all the needles went. Only one time did it feel uncomfortable, and that was in a spot somewhere on my left foot. I have heard that to some, feet can be very sensual. I've never subscribed to this, as I have a second toe that looks like a foot-long hot dog and protrudes way beyond my big toe. This sight being quite bizarre, I have never encouraged any sexual partner to wander down near my dangling dogs. In the acupuncture world, however, the feet talk to the shmirshky. Good to know.

The very best part of the acupuncture hour is the massage you get while the needles are in (be sure to ask for this). I believe I was carried away somewhere far from PM&M land. I noticed my body sinking into the bed and my extremities becoming like J-e-l-l-O—all smooshy and gooshy and wonderful. I didn't want to leave. I paid for this wonderful service and floated out of the office.*

---

* I dished out $80 for this fabulous experience, but costs will vary depending on the practitioner and length of the session. Be sure to check with your insurance providers, as many carriers cover acupuncture these days.

let my shmirshky go

Remember me, the Master Organizer? Well, apparently I had one humongous messy drawer with stuff bulging out of it that I had neglected for years. I know it's a shocker. After all, my closet is organized by color and clothing type, and each hanger is facing the same direction. All the towels in my linen closet are perfectly folded and aligned by size and color. Nothing in my house is messy; I am always ready to have a party at the drop of a hat; no special cleaning needed! I never leave my house without making my bed. My mom assured me that this is very important. After all, someone could stop by! In the thirty-nine years since I moved out of my mother's home, no one has ever stopped by and gone into my bedroom—not even her. Still, I am always ready.

So, please explain to me how the Supreme Master Organizer of the Universe had a messy drawer *anywhere*.

The answer is simple: the messy drawer was in my head. You see, I had spent many years choosing to focus on others' needs and emotions, leaving no time to focus on my own. It was so much easier being there for others than it was being there for myself. I am way more of a handful.

Once again, I found PM&M teaching me many new things. I had no choice but to open up this drawer, as all kinds of emotions had started bursting out of it. The crazier my hormones were, the more difficult it was for me to keep this drawer closed. Oh, yes, I tried. I mentally shoved a gigantic, heavy chair under the knob, but it didn't work. So I decided to let it all out. Yes, you have to take *everything* out, one item at a time. There are no shortcuts to this. If you empty only half the drawer, the other half will still be a bursting mess.

Here is how I did it. Every evening I took a wonderful, relaxing bath. It was here that I was completely alone. Surrounded by my bath salts and bubbles, I carefully opened my bulging drawer. I took out one emotion at a time and let myself feel. These feelings were a part of me. I needed to acknowledge and respect them. Most of my life I only knew how to be Type A, but now I was learning how to just B!*

Some nights I cried. Some nights I laughed. Some nights I was angry and disappointed. Most important, I allowed myself to not be "fine." I realized many new things about myself—some that I liked, some that I wanted to change. Change is good.

Shmirshkies are brought up to be the caregivers, but we *must* learn how to think inside the box and take care of ourselves. Find your own special time and place to go through your drawer. It takes time, so be patient and love yourself through the process. Not everything you've done will look or feel so

---

* Type A people are known for their impatience, aggressiveness, and competitiveness. Who, me? Type B folks, by contrast, are known for having a lack of aggressiveness and tension. Sounds glorious!

good in retrospect, but that's okay—no one is perfect. Love and respect the old you, just as you embrace the new.

By the way, there's no need to put all that stuff back in the drawer! No folding neatly or organizing by color. Practice tackling the emotions as they arise. If the drawer starts to build up again, go back and clean it out. Try going through your drawer each night (maybe after you brush your teeth). If you find that there are a few big issues in that drawer that require a professional organizer, don't be afraid to find a counselor to help you.

We need to learn how to be comfortable with being *vulnerable*. I found that when I allowed myself to be vulnerable, I became fearless. A fearless shmirshky is a wonderful thing!

sumo free

So many times I felt alone during PM&M, except, of course, for the sumo wrestler in my head. You know the massive wrestlers who wear those *mawashi* loincloths? A guy like *that*! He is big. I mean, really, *really* big and very intimidating. In real life they might be nice guys, but in my mind, my sumo is always saying horrible things to me, like:

✳ You're getting old and wrinkled.

✳ You'll never sleep well again.

✳ You're already fat, so you might as well finish all that cookie dough and skip baking the cookies.

✳ You're not smart anymore.

✳ You're not sexy anymore.

✳ You'd better fix this PM&M.

✳ You'd better get this book done fast and make it perfect!

You want to hear something crazy? My sumo never wrestles me down. He never even touches me. I just fall down all by myself! Who gives him all this power? Why is he in charge? I've spent so much wasted time listening to my sumo. Apparently, he has been in there a long time—way too long. Recently, I was going through old scrapbooks, and I realized that I have never been happy with my body. Even as teenagers running around in bikinis, my girlfriends and I always thought we were fat. I look at old pictures now and think I was nuts. Most of us shmirshkies act like it's *our job to feel fat* our whole lives. Now when I look at myself in the mirror, I think, "I am FF!" (Fucking Fabulous! Sorry, Mom.)

To top it all off, many of us seem to be experts at not having a good relationship with food. I abused my food terribly. I would grab a huge container of ice cream and scarf it down. When I ate that first scoop or bite of raw cookie dough or that cupcake, it was so yummy! But when I power ate, I was in an abusive relationship with my food. I know it sounds silly, but PM&M helped me to take a look at this dysfunctional relationship in my life. Now I try to treat my food with kindness, like I do my other relationships. No more *mean eating*!

--------------------- shmirshky party alert!

Y I was curious if everyone had a sumo. Do you remember my friend Patty? She's a stunning, sweet, ex-ballerina, retired entrepreneur, culinary master, multilinguist, and voracious reader (it's important that you understand her extraordinary talents before you read her answer). Her answer sounded pretty familiar. "I was always a perfectionist and most of my life I felt confident that what I was doing was good. As I got older, my sumo got stronger. As fashion and appearance, weight and leg length became bigger issues, my sumo grew in power. As a dancer, my legs were too short and too big; at least, that's what my sumo told me. During PM&M, my looks and behavior began to change and I grew less and less confident in myself. I became more susceptible to sumo influence and much more insecure with everything I did or said. Tread lightly, sumo in session!"

Y I asked Debbi the same question and she said, "Wrestling down my sumo is a full-time job. Sometimes I win, sometimes my sumo wins."

Often, when I'm battling my sumo, I remind myself of my friend Yvette. Yvette had a very flamboyant, artsy kind of style. You would often see her in top hats, feathers, and large, funky jewelry. We would have lunch at least twice a week and talk on the phone every day. There was never a time that Yvette didn't mention how unhappy she was with her weight and her wrinkles. In my eyes, she was a beautiful shmirshky with passion, boundless energy, and a one-of-a-kind style. I often wished that I could have helped her to see what I saw.

It never happened. Yvette was diagnosed with a very serious and aggressive form of cancer. Toward the end, she could no longer eat a thing. She became so thin and frail; she was wasting away. I thought about all those years Yvette had spent being self-critical. We all do it. Toward the end of her time, Yvette would have given anything to be able to gain weight and get more wrinkled. I remind myself of this often when I'm putting on my makeup and my sumo reappears. Sumo, be gone!

Being aware of your sumo is so helpful because he shows up a lot! Now when my sumo jumps in my face and begins yelling at me, I try to minimize him—I make him smaller in my mind. Over time, he keeps shrinking. He's a tiny sumo now, not nearly as scary. Try living every day SUMO FREE!

the sisterhood
of the shrinking pants

It doesn't matter if you start out as a size 0 or a size 20; your body is going to change. I'm quite sure that one night while I was sleeping, the PM&M alien came and put my body in a blender and turned it on high. Nothing is where it used to be. I also thought the alien was shrinking my clothes. My wardrobe seemed to be getting smaller and smaller! This happens to almost every PM&M shmirshky I talk to. *It is not your fault.* Your body slows down, and at the same time you find yourself depressed. So what does a gal do when she is down? Eat bad carbs, of course! Bad carbs love PM&M shmirshkies. They stick on your body and won't let go. I heard the sumo yelling at me, "Eat all these carbs now!"

Before I knew it, I was gravitating toward the looser clothes in my wardrobe. I noticed I was wearing the same things over and over again. Why didn't anyone tell me about PM&M earlier, when I was pregnant? I would have saved some of those loose tops, dresses, and pants with the stretchy fabric over the belly.

My clothes were getting dusty! Most of them had not seen the light of day in a long, long time. I began trying every diet in the book along with cranking my workouts up to high intensity.

I should have been a pencil, but instead I was even hungrier and the buttons on my clothes were still popping!

Since we live in a society that is obsessed with weight, many shmirshkies turn to diet and exercise as a way to drop pounds during PM&M. Of course, everyone's body is different: some shmirshkies find that healthy eating and regular exercise make a big impact on their weight, and others, like me, end up frustrated by disappointing results. Many of us are so fixated on losing weight that we forget about what is actually healthy for our bodies and our minds.

Don't let your sumo set the goals. My sumo wants me to look like I'm sixteen again, and that's just not fair! Instead, make it about how you *feel*. While I don't always look forward to working out, I always feel great after I finish.* My aerobic exercise of choice is bike riding. Many mornings, you will find me riding around my neighborhood on my orange bike (my fave color). I smile and say hi to people as I ride by, and most days I get a smile and hello back. This way, I start my day on an upbeat and get my exercise in at the same time. On weekends, I try to change it up and take power walks that are fast enough to get my heart rate going.

Whether you like to swim, hike, run, play sports, or do yoga, find workout methods that are fun and work for you. The point isn't to be the next supermodel, but rather to *feel* good

---

* Aerobic exercise releases endorphins, which make us feel good—even euphoric. I love these endorphins; they are really something! As it turns out, exercise is just as important for your mental and emotional health as it is for your physical health. It can help ward off depression, increase your daily energy, and help you sleep better.

and improve your overall health and well-being. If you don't like working out alone, find a buddy and support each other. If diet and exercise become a source of stress, then you're defeating the purpose. Take the pressure off and reevaluate your goals so they're positive and realistic. Healthy eating and regular exercise should be gifts you give to yourself. Who doesn't love getting lavished with gifts?

Unfortunately, losing weight can become an obsession for PM&M shmirshkies and there are no cookie-cutter solutions (although avoiding the cookies isn't a bad idea). I didn't lose a pound until I got my thyroid and hormones balanced. If you're like me and find that PM&M has made you a member of the sisterhood of the shrinking pants, I have *great* news—there are some magic answers to this problem:

✳ The extra-large plastic garbage bag

✳ Spanx

✳ A seamstress

First, go buy a box of the largest plastic garbage bags you can find. Fill up the bags with all those clothes that don't fit anymore and get rid of all that dust. My days were so much more joyful when I wasn't looking at those damn clothes every day. When I finally did this, I felt like I had scored one for the PM&M shmirshky. I didn't want to waste another day being unhappy and grumpy by wearing pants that choked off the circulation to my shmirshky. No, I did not! I *did* have a choice.

This was so liberating! Save the bags in your storage closet or garage as you might be able to fit back into *some* of these things later. In the meantime, I went out and bought a couple of pairs of pants that fit me. I didn't care what the hell size they were. I needed to feel comfortable. I threw in a few loose tops and dresses, and I was a new shmirshky. Yes, I was!

The second amazing invention you must arm yourself with is Spanx (spanx.com). Spanx are "designed by a woman and are crafted to promote comfort and confidence in women." They're sold everywhere. You wear them under your clothes to smooth out your figure. Think of them as a reverse balloon. Instead of blowing out and filling up, you're sucking in and smoothing down. They're incredible! At first, I thought that the smaller the Spanx, the better I would look. No! No! No! Do not buy Spanx so small that you break out in a sweat just struggling to pull them up. If you do, you will have a *huge spillover* at the waist—and this is not the kind of spillover that you can mop up with your Pap smear paper towel. Plus, you will *not* be fun to be with if you can't breathe. In fact, you will be a bitch on wheels. Remember, you got rid of the clothes that cut off your circulation for a reason.

Finally, if you have some special clothes that you can't get yourself to put in the large garbage bag or fit into with Spanx, get out your sewing kit or find a seamstress. Once during PM&M, I needed to go to a black-tie party. I usually couldn't wait to get all dressed up, but this time I was stalling. I put off going into the closet until the very last minute. As you may have already figured out, last minute is not my usual MO. I eventually ventured into my closet and, yes, you guessed it—not one of my long gowns fit me, even with the "extra hold" Spanx! I sent out an SOS to a dear friend of mine for a recommendation of a good seamstress. I'd never met this seamstress before. Here I was, a new customer, and I needed to get a gown fixed in one day. I explained that I was having a PM&M crisis. I did not have to say another thing. She immediately understood and fixed the dress for me. The Sisterhood to the rescue, presto change-o!

Oh, and one last thing I almost forgot: when you're not plucking out stray chin hairs, turn off the lights on that magnifying mirror you use to put on your makeup. You know what I'm talking about, the one that makes you feel like you're being interrogated by a seventh grader in biology class. Who invented that? So unnecessary! Shut down those unflattering lights. It feels so good to be in charge again!

shmirshky board

There are so many wonderful people in our lives, but often, when we don't feel good about ourselves, our sumo takes control and keeps us from letting them in. Yes, the sumo wants to keep the PM&M shmirshky all to himself . . . just hanging out, eating bad carbs, and staying miserable. Oh, joy! There were many days when I just didn't want to see anyone or go anywhere; I didn't want to wear real clothes (whoever invented the bathrobe, thank you!); I didn't want to have to fake a smile; I didn't want to pretend everything was "fine." These lonely and depressing days often seem like life's only option.

Don't worry, you are not alone. Your gynecologist is your partner in the shmirshky business, and your advocate is by your side at those special doctor visits. Additionally, you have a Shmirshky Board (SB) to accompany you through your PM&M adventure. Picture all the people closest to you in your life, sitting around a big boardroom table, ready to help you through this challenging time. They need to understand what you are going through, and it's your job as chairshmirshky of the board to let them in. Your SB might include your children, parents, grandparents, dear friends, coworkers, girlfriend, boyfriend, soul mate, or lover. Who is on your SB?

Many of our SB members don't have a clue as to what is going on with us when we hit PM&M. They don't know why we are acting distant and irritable. They don't understand the changes we are experiencing. Often, a lack of communication about PM&M results in serious strains in our important relationships and can lead to tragic and unnecessary divisions. Do not hide! Instead, go seek out the love and support you deserve from the shmirshkies and erlicks you love, respect, and trust.

———————— shmirshky party alert!

Theresa's approach for assembling her SB is quite evolved. "The nice thing about getting older is that I've learned to appreciate people for what they have to offer and not to expect more, so that is why I cast my net wide." I love that! Being a wise shmirshky isn't about having all the answers, it's about recognizing when you need support and knowing where and how to get the help you need.

Theresa's SB consists of her three sisters (as she puts it, "If you weren't given a great sister, go find one!"), her husband, a couple wonderful business colleagues (they support each other both professionally and personally), three friends from college, her sister-in-law, and her Gay Husband! In addition, she uses meditation to get herself out of a funk or a pickle and she calls a shrink when she needs a tune-up. Theresa is one smart shmirshky!

Push aside your sumo and pull your SB closer to you. Reach out to them! Allow yourself to be vulnerable and admit that you are having a tough time. They do not have a crystal ball that can read your shmirshky. Think of how clear the message would be if we just gave it to them straight and honest. Practice saying, "I am having problems and need your help." You can do it! Then help them understand what you are going through. Give them books (this one would be good!) or guide them to the Web sites that you found helpful. Talk to them, lean on them, share your challenges and feelings, and eliminate all of the confusion around PM&M.

It is amazing how much better I felt when I was open and honest with my SB. By the way, there is no official boardroom needed. You can meet for coffee or dinner, grab a sandwich or go for a walk, talk on the phone or work out with your SB while you're meeting. It feels good to not be alone. Reaching out is IN. Suffering in silence is OUT!

shmirshky
don't-jump-off-a-cliff notes

If you're a shmirshky and you're lucky enough to get older, you will experience PM&M. PM&M is not a disease. It is a part of each and every shmirshky's journey. I hope this book helps you, a loved one, a partner-shmirshky, or an important erlick in your life to understand PM&M. Be *pro*active about your health instead of *re*active, and remember to think inside the box. We don't go *through* PM&M, as I had originally thought, but rather, we *are* PM&M!

Here's the condensed shmirshky:

✳ The period. Who knew a dot could be such a handful? When we're young, we can't wait to get it! We spend half of our lives amongst a sea of period paraphernalia with strings, cardboard, sticks, and wings swarming all around our bathrooms, backpacks, purses, and suitcases. After years of the period, we find ourselves fantasizing about life without it: sounds dreamy.

✳ PM&M doesn't fit neatly into a quick and simple definition. As children, we're taught (if at all) to assume that PM&M is just something that happens without much fanfare or a big to-do. I WISH!

✳ Shmirshky alert! The storm is brewing. Every shmirshky is different, so you can't really Google "shmirshky weather" for an exact forecast. For some, it feels like a hurricane, for others, little raindrops. Either way, you need an umbrella or your bush will get all wet.

✳ During PM&M, you may feel like an alien swooped down, took over your body, and jumbled up your mind and personality . . . not to mention your hips, your boobs, and your waist. The list goes on and on! Don't worry; odds are that you aren't actually losing your mind!

✳ The PM&M shmirshky has been suffering in silence for far too long. Let's bust open the shmirshky cover-up. PM&M is not a curse or a crime. We must acknowledge that this is going to be a challenging time, and that's okay. We don't always have to be "fine"!

✳ PM&M begins when you are young and active, but you won't get a save-the-date to keep on your refrigerator. There's no telling when it will start, and every shmirshky is different. Be prepared and you won't feel like you're suddenly at a black-tie reception dressed for a football game.

✳ Do not hide your shmirshky under a bush! If we're open with each other about PM&M, then we can be prepared for the difficulties that lie ahead. Here are a few things to keep in your PM&M Prep Kit: sticky notes; tweezers; a hand fan; your Shmirshky Journal (see page 171); your SB on speed dial; a change of clothes; a whole lot of patience, love, and understanding; and a tampon (just in case).

✳ For all those PM&M shmirshkies who can't sleep, you are not alone! Many shmirshkies define sleepless nights as one of their most nagging symptoms. I love the movie *Sleepless in Seattle*, but Sleepless in PM&M is neither cute nor romantic!

✳ Are you a hyper/hypo? Many shmirshkies find that they have a thyroid condition at the onset of PM&M. Thyroid conditions and PM&M symptoms are very similar. This can be confusing to the already discombobulated PM&M shmirshky. Be sure to get your TSH checked!

✳ PM&M shmirshkies are a very hot group! Your days and nights may involve lots of sweat sessions and hot flushes. This is only temporary. Trust me; there are dripless days in your future.

✳ Do your own shmirshky recon and learn about PM&M. Browse the PM&M section at your local bookstore. There are some wonderful shmirshky magazines to check out as well. If you aren't in the mood to take off your bathrobe, go online and order the books you need and have them delivered right to your door.

✳ Finding a great doctor is so important. Gather doctor recommendations and research them thoroughly. Use all the resources available to you: friends, family, other doctors, and the Internet. Think of yourself as a shmirshky private "I"!

✳ Interview the doctors you've found before making a decision. Have your advocate and your Shmirshky Daily Symptoms Chart (page 168) in tow. Remember, your gynecologist is your partner, and you want to be able to ask questions and be okay with *not* being "fine"! Make sure you are comfortable with the way the office is run and the style and approach of the doctor. If you find that you chose a doctor who isn't working for you, don't be afraid to switch. You deserve the best!

✳ Once you have educated yourself and selected your doctor, find out what your numbers are. Ask for all the tests that you need. Take your advocate with you and sit down with your doctor. Look over the lab results in detail. Be honest about how you *feel*. Discuss in detail all of the options available to you. (Don't forget shmirshky's next-door neighbor. You might be at the age when you need a colonoscopy too!) Maybe someday soon, all our shmirshky tests will be noninvasive. No more poking and smooshing!

✳ The big question is whether to HRT [*] or not to HRT. Read about the WHI[✢] and learn about its findings. There is a Hormone Therapy Menu on page 154 (no dessert on this menu, unfortunately). Understand the options available to you and talk about these choices with your doctor and SB.[✖] Remember—whether you do HRT or not, it will be a process. It's not black and white; rather, it's a trial-and-error kind of experience. Be patient. You *will* find the answers. It all comes down to *your quality of life*. Think inside the box. If you listen carefully, your body will talk to you.

✳ Host a Shmirshky Party! The Sisterhood may have great resources or doctors to recommend. If you share your experiences, they will share back. If you give them a cocktail, they will share more! You can find all kinds of fun Shmirshky Party tips, including a recipe for the Shmirshky Cosmo, at shmirshky.com. While you're there, reach out to the network of shmirshkies and erlicks on the blog and message board. After all, reaching out is IN. Suffering in silence is OUT!

---

[*] Hormone replacement therapy; also called HT (hormone therapy or hormone treatment).
[✢] Women's Health Initiative
[✖] Shmirshky Board

✳ The period is quite the drama queen—never able to really decide whether or not to leave. Who knew that the period would love such dramatic good-byes? Enough already! A simple peck on the cheek would have been terrific. Be patient as the Period Queen makes her exit. Don't be surprised if she pops back in before she finally leaves for good.

✳ Sometimes I wished I had an erlick, because it seemed like life would have been so much easier. The truth is, erlicks have their fair share of health challenges. If you think you're living with Grumpy (and you're no Snow White), your favorite erlick might be experiencing male menopause. Too bad there aren't two-for-one deals at your local blood lab.

✳ Don't give up. I hope this book will help you hit the shmirshky jackpot early, so you don't suffer alone and without the proper support. No matter how long it takes for you to feel better, don't lose hope. You are worth the effort!

✳ Redecorating the shmirshky is not something to take lightly. If your doctor recommends a hysterectomy, be sure to get more than one opinion before booking the surgery. If you find that it's your only option, do your own research and learn about the various types of surgeries and their potential side effects. Go over the options with your doctor and select the procedure that best fits your needs.

✳ While you are handling the many challenges of the PM&M shmirshky, you may find that your shmirshky has moved to the Mojave Desert. Yes, your shmirshky is hot *and* parched! Don't feel ashamed! There are many options available to you, so be open with your partner and your doctor. An oasis is right around the corner!

✳ Many PM&M shmirshkies use acupuncture with great success. Don't worry; they don't put any needles in your shmirshky, so give it a whirl. Be sure to ask for the massage too. That was my favorite part.

✳ Let your shmirshky go! Take everything out of that bulging emotional drawer. It can be a long process, but it is well worth the effort. There's no need to stuff emotions away any longer. Experience them and let them be. Think of how much lighter you'll feel!

✳ Banish the sumo in your mind! Everybody has one, but when you're living SUMO FREE, it's really the most amazing way to be!

✳ Bag up the clothes that don't fit and make you feel horrible. No need to torture yourself anymore. Instead of focusing on how you look, focus on how you feel. Give yourself the gift of fun exercise and healthy eating. Love your body. You are beautiful just the way you are, even if PM&M changes things around a bit. Yes, you may find that during the different stages of PM&M there might be more of you to love. What's wrong with that? Eventually you might find that you can open some of those bags back up and enjoy the clothes again!

✳ Shmirshky business is big business. You need a Shmirshky Board to help love and support you. Your SB members are the people you're around the most; you might even live with a few of them. If you share your PM&M experience with them, they can be understanding and comforting. Don't hold back. Remember, they don't have a crystal ball that tells them how you're feeling. I know you're accustomed to being the caregiver, but it's your turn now.

There is a light at the end of this deep, seemingly dark tunnel. I had to get a huge flashlight and search for it, but it's there, I promise. I am passing along my flashlight to you! The light helped me to see myself better. While I am still learning, laughing, and crying with other shmirshkies, I do not feel like an alien has taken over my body anymore. It is mine, and I love who I am now. I hear my own shmirshky choir. Yes, it is big! Dozens and dozens of shmirshkies all singing, embracing, and celebrating PM&M!

I hope this book brings you a little bit of the three L's: love, laughter, and learning. Throughout this process, I learned so much, not just about the person I am becoming but also about the person that I've been. So thank you, PM&M, for all you have taught me. It was certainly a surprise to have you as a teacher.

the period

afterglow

my shmirshky

I have included a section at the end of this book entitled "My Shmirshky Journal." Use these pages to begin writing about *your* experiences. You can pass the book and your wisdom along to your friends or family. Think of it as a family heirloom, shmirshky style.

Writing might feel a bit strange at first, but don't worry, that's normal. Initially, I found that expressing myself in written form was very scary. Over the years my children had bought me the most beautiful journals. I always put them by my bed, hoping that one day I would feel comfortable enough to pick one up and begin writing. Every time I glanced over at the empty journals piled neatly on my nightstand, I made a mental note to write in one of them. Instead of collecting my thoughts, all they seemed to do was collect dust.

Then it happened. It was time. I sat down and started writing about my PM&M experience. My hand was cramping and my fingers couldn't write fast enough, so I moved to the computer to type. Thoughts, feelings, and questions started to pour out of me. I just let myself go. I wanted to get it *all* down. Writing helped to ease the loneliness and sadness that I was experiencing. Writing was just like talking, and I'm happy to report that I can do both now. Go ahead, get in your comfy robe and give it a try! Your PM&M story could be a great gift for the shmirshkies and erlicks in your life.

If you feel like chatting, go to shmirshky.com and join in the conversation. I am happy to listen, laugh, cry, and learn with you as you too embrace PM&M in the pursuit of hormone happiness.

happy birthday!

To my SB: *

> my most cherished erlick, my husband, David;
>
> my remarkable son, Jack, who collaborated with me on
> *Shmirshky* and is my Shmirshky Universal partner
> and so much more! Thank you for contributing your
> extraordinary blend of writing talent and comedic
> genius;
>
> my most treasured shmirshky, my sounding board on all
> things shmirshky, my daughter and dearest friend,
> Sarah;
>
> my loving mother, who always has my vaccination records
> handy;
>
> my father, who is always with me;
>
> and my beloved BFF, Marcia.

To my *Shmirshky* Magellan, Ellen Archer, for discovering
Shmirshky and bringing it to the world.

To my *Shmirshky* editor, Barbara Jones. I would never put my
Shmirshky in anyone else's hands (except David's).

---

* Shmirshky Board

To my *Shmirshky* literary agents, Trena Keating and Sally Wofford-Girand. What can I say, you lit up my life.

To the rest of the amazing Hyperion/VOICE team of special operatives: Anna Campbell, Marie Coolman, Brenda Copeland, Molly Frandson, Caroline Grill, Maha Khalil, Kristin Kiser, Sharon Kitter, Laura Klynstra, Joan Lee, Allison McGeehon, Claire McKean, Karen Minster, Mike Rotondo, Sarah Rucker, Jill Sansone, Katherine Tasheff, and Betsy Wilson.

To my SS, Ivy Van-Allen. You and your Jack inspire me!

To my *Shmirshky* design guru, Marika van Adelsberg. You make my *Shmirshky* look so good.

To my original *Shmirshky* book doctors: Jack Dolgen (Chief of Surgery), Gregory Dobie, Rachel Haimowitz, Sarah Hagan, Ceebs Bailey, and Shaina Friel.

To all my helpful shmirshkies and erlicks: Leo Ammann, Wanda Aurich, Nate Becker, Jenny Bennett, Abigail Berman, Judy Berman, Arik Betesh, Tony Bever, Marlena Bittner, Melanie Bivens, Michelle Blincoe, Lynne M. J. Boisineau, Sarah Bro, Denise Brodey, Jennie Brook, Gail and Ralph Bryan, Chris Burns, Tina Byrnes, Carin and Hillary Canale-Theakston, Cristina Castillo, Kris Chang, Linda Chester, Michael Claggett, Robyn Cohen, Gayle Cole, Ruth Corech, Ian Corson, Jay Corson, Marc Dahm, Nia Davis, Janice Dodge, Jonathan Dolgen, Lauren Dolgen, Susan Drescher-Mulzet, Dr. Daniel Einhorn, Emily Einhorn, Dr. James Evers, Marissa Faith,

Eric J. Feig, Michele Ferrebeuf, Carolina Finch, Laurent Fischer, Elaine and Murray Galinson, Cindy Gallop, Joe Gartner, Morris Gearring, Katherine Gehl, Christine Givant, Curtis Gwinn, Francesca Harewood, Karen Hensler, Deb Hubers, Tiffany Hughes, Harrison Hurwitz, Steven Hyde, Bonnie and Peter Jones, Larry Katz, Robin Kay, Wendy Kelman, Dr. Joseph Kennedy, Derek Kent, Jillian Kirk, Robin Kirk, Kathryn Kogge, Lorna LaRiviere, Whitney Lasky, Ina Manaster, Doug Mand, Dr. Michael Maywood, Ken McClellan, Brian McDonough, Jane McPherson, Pauline Metzler, Mike Monaghan, Mark Mulzet, Priscilla Nicholas, Melanie and John Nogawski, Kathleen Pacurar, Adam Pally, Nicole Pearl, Laurel Pfannenstiel, Steve Poe, Toni Pollack, Julie Potash, Mike Pruter, Jillian Puglisi, Dr. Ted Quigley, Mojgan Rady, Mike Regan, Patti Regan, Tanya Rietz, Kristen Rodack, Juju Rodriguez, Marian Rosenberg, Verne Rosenfield, Ryan Rossiter, Kathleen Santin, Phyllis Savage, Char Self, Suzan and Gad Shaanan, Debbie Shiflett, Gail Shoultes, Ben Sinclair, Marcia Skidmore, Andrew Spurgin, Angela Stanley, Dale Steele, Mimi Tackaberry, Gayle and Phil Tauber, Susan Topol, Greg Tuculescu, Beth Vesel, Maria Villalobos, Lauren Weissman, Pamela Whitcomb, Amy Wiborg, Kitty and Keen Wolcott, Hilda Wynn, and Greg Zola.

To my cozy robe, coffee cup, and martini.

To my PM&M!

shmirshky fun terms

Term	Definition	Page
BFF	Birthday Friend Forever	vi
erlick	Penis; man; male; dude	1
erlickogram	Luckily for the erlicks, this doesn't exist!	85
FF	Fucking Fabulous!	106
Gay Husband	This is someone who not only gives you all the love and support of a husband but also enjoys shopping and getting mani-pedis, *and* knows how to throw a fabulous party.	40
HS	Hot Shmirshky; a shmirshky feeling the hot flashes!	39
"I'm fine"	The motto of the shmirshky cover-up; what you might hear shouted out from under a bush: "I'm fine!"	19
M	Menopause	1
MTZ	Menstruation Twilight Zone	7
PM	Perimenopause	1
PM&M	The entire time in a shmirshky's life when she's going through the menopause experience (that includes the pre, the peri, and the post!)	1

Term	Definition	Page
PM&M Prep Kit	Sticky notes; tweezers; a hand fan; your My Shmirshky Journal; your SB on speed dial; a change of clothes; a whole lot of patience, love, and understanding; and a tampon (just in case)	28/ 121
SB	Shmirshky Board: you know your SB members, you probably see them every day!	115
shmirshky	Vagina; woman; female; babe	1
Shmirshky Party	Whenever shmirshkies share their experiences with each other. This often includes cocktails, laughter, and love. Visit shmirshky.com to find fun tips for your next Shmirshky Party.	123
Sisterhood of Shmirshkies	All the ladies near and far	4
Sumo	The hypercritical voice inside your head	105
SUMO FREE	A great way to be!	108

Term	Definition	Page
think inside the box	When you're in PM&M, you've got to think inside the box! Think about how you feel, listen to your body, and recognize your needs. Prioritize and trust yourself as a shmirshky. Sometimes erlicks need to think inside the box as well, albeit in a different way than they usually do.	3

shmirshky not-so-fun terms*

Term	Definition	Page
acupuncture	A practice developed in China of inserting fine needles through the skin at specific points to cure disease or relieve pain. http://nccam.nih.gov/health/ acupuncture/introduction.htm	97
Alzheimer's disease	A form of dementia. It's a progressive, degenerative brain disease that affects one's capacity for memory and thought. http://www.nlm.nih.gov/medlineplus/ ency/article/000760.htm	11
bioidentical hormones	A bioidentical hormone is identical to the hormone produced in your body. It may not have originated in your body, but it has the same chemical structure and even goes by the same name. Most important, it has the same biological function. http://www.medterms.com/script/main/ art.asp?articlekey=98553	66

---

* All Web sites in the Shmirshky Not-So-Fun Terms support both the definitions listed in this section as well as the matching definitions in the text and footnotes of the book (see page numbers) and were retrieved on October 9, 2010, unless otherwise specified.

Term	Definition	Page
bone density	The measure of calcium and other minerals in your bones. http://www.nlm.nih.gov/medlineplus/ency/article/007197.htm	58
CA-125	Cancer antigen 125; best known as a blood marker for ovarian cancer. It may also be elevated with other malignant cancers, including those originating in the endometrium, fallopian tubes, lungs, breasts, and gastrointestinal tract. http://www.nlm.nih.gov/medlineplus/ency/article/007217.htm http://www.nlm.nih.gov/medlineplus/ency/article/000889.htm	59
cholesterol	A waxy substance produced by the body. It is needed to make hormones, skin cells, and digestive juices. http://www.nlm.nih.gov/medlineplus/ency/article/003492.htm	60
cholesterol/HDL	The ratio of total cholesterol to HDL. http://www.americanheart.org/presenter.jhtml?identifier=4503	60

Term	Definition	Page
colonoscopy	An examination of the large colon and part of the small bowel with a curious little camera they stick up shmirshky and erlick's next-door neighbor. (Is this more fun than a Pap smear? Have one of each and then decide.) http://www.nlm.nih.gov/medlineplus/ency/article/003886.htm	85
compounding pharmacy	These pharmacies create medication formulas, specifically designed for a particular individual's needs. http://www.iacprx.org/site/PageServer?pagename=What_is_Compounding	155
DEXA	Dual energy X-ray absorptiometry; a test to measure the bone density (strength) of both the hip and spine. http://www.osteopenia3.com/dexa-scans.html	58
DHEAS	Dehydroepiandrosterone sulfate; a hormone that is easily converted into other hormones, including estrogen and testosterone. DHEAS is the sulfated (S) form of DHEA in the blood. http://www.medterms.com/script/main/art.asp?articlekey=25613	60

Term	Definition	Page
early menopause	Currently the cutoff for early menopause is forty-five, which means a shmirshky has been without her period for twelve consecutive months at the age of forty-five or younger. This can happen naturally or as a result of surgery. http://www.menopause.org/Portals/0/Content/PDF/A.pdf	26
endocrinologist	A medical expert specializing in the diseases of the endocrine system (glands and hormones). http://www.hormone.org/public/endocrinologist.cfm	35
endometriosis	A condition in which the tissue that behaves like the cells lining the uterus grows in other areas of the body (usually in the pelvic area, outside the uterus, on the ovaries, bowel, rectum, or bladder). http://www.nlm.nih.gov/medlineplus/ency/article/000915.htm	92
estradiol	The most important form of estrogen produced in the body. http://www.nlm.nih.gov/medlineplus/ency/article/003711.htm	71

Term	Definition	Page
estriol	The weakest of the three main types of estrogen. http://www.merriam-webster.com/dictionary/estriol	71
estrogen	The primary female hormone. Estrogen is responsible for the development and maintenance of female reproductive structures. http://www2.merriam-webster.com/cgi-bin/mwmednlm?book=medical&va=estrogen	59
estrogen dominance	When there's too much estrogen relative to progesterone in a shmirshky's body. Heavy bleeding and sometimes even cancer can result from this.	73
estrone	One of the three most common types of estrogen secreted by the ovaries (the other two are estradiol and estriol). http://www.labtestsonline.org/understanding/analytes/estrogen/test.html	71

Term	Definition	Page
FDA	The Food and Drug Administration; a federal agency that oversees the safety regulations of most types of food, supplements, drugs, vaccines, and medical products. http://www.fda.gov	69
FSH	Follicle stimulating hormone; a pituitary hormone that stimulates the growth of the ovum (the egg and surrounding cells that produce ovarian hormones). This is one of the measures that can indicate if you've entered M (although it's not a definitive determinant because your levels can fluctuate). http://www.nlm.nih.gov/medlineplus/ ency/article/003710.htm	62
Grave's disease	An autoimmune disorder that affects the thyroid gland and leads to thyroid hyperactivity (hyperthyroidism). http://www.nlm.nih.gov/medlineplus/ ency/article/000358.htm	34
gynecologist	A doctor specializing in the business of the shmirshky.	47

Term	Definition	Page
Hashimoto's disease	Also called chronic lymphocytic thyroiditis. The immune system attacks the thyroid gland, which causes inflammation and leads to an underactive thyroid (hypothyroidism). http://www.nlm.nih.gov/medlineplus/ency/article/000371.htm	34
HDL	High-density lipoprotein; the "good" cholesterol. http://www.nlm.nih.gov/medlineplus/ency/article/003496.htm	60
HRT	Hormone replacement therapy; also called HT (hormone therapy or hormone treatment). HRT is a supplement of hormones to treat the symptoms of PM&M. The hormones are commonly estrogen, progesterone, and testosterone. http://www.nlm.nih.gov/medlineplus/ency/article/007111.htm	66

Term	Definition	Page
hyperthyroidism	Hyperthyroidism, or an overactive thyroid gland, is usually caused by the autoimmune illness called Grave's disease. In this condition, the body's immune system produces an antibody that stimulates the gland to make an excess amount of T3 and T4, the two forms of thyroid hormone. (The 3 and the 4 refer to the number of iodines in that form of the hormone.) If you're a "hyper," you may experience some of these symptoms: enlarged thyroid gland (goiter), bulging eyes, sudden weight loss, rapid heartbeat, increased appetite, nervousness and anxiety, irritability, tremor in the hands and fingers, sweating, changes in menstrual patterns, increased sensitivity to heat, more frequent bowel movements, and difficulty sleeping. http://www.nlm.nih.gov/medlineplus/ency/article/000356.htm	34

Term	Definition	Page
hypothyroidism	Hypothyroidism is usually caused by Hashimoto's disease. The thyroid gland doesn't produce enough thyroid hormone, which slows down the body's metabolism. If you're a "hypo," you may experience weight gain, increased sensitivity to cold, dry skin and hair, slow pulse, low blood pressure, constipation, depressed mood, muscle aches/weakness, hair loss, low energy, and all kinds of sluggishness. http://www.nlm.nih.gov/medlineplus/ency/article/000353.htm	34
hysterectomy	An operation in which the uterus is removed. http://www.nlm.nih.gov/medlineplus/ency/article/002915.htm	89
incontinence	Incontinence refers to the loss of bladder control. For shmirshkies, this can mean anything from mild drips to full-on floods. http://www.nlm.nih.gov/medlineplus/urinaryincontinence.html	90
LDL	Low-density lipoprotein; the "bad" cholesterol. Too much LDL in the blood can clog your arteries. http://www.nlm.nih.gov/medlineplus/ency/article/003495.htm	60

Term	Definition	Page
male menopause	The term *male menopause* is a bit misleading, since erlicks don't have a menstrual cycle. What male menopause typically refers to is the decrease in testosterone levels in middle-aged men, often resulting in menopause-like symptoms including fatigue, depression, physical weakness, and a lower libido. http://www.mayoclinic.com/health/male-menopause/MC00058	83
mammogram	An X-ray picture of the breasts. It is used to find tumors and to help tell the difference between non-cancerous (benign) and cancerous (malignant) disease. http://www.nlm.nih.gov/medlineplus/ency/article/003380.htm	57

Term	Definition	Page
menopause	The time in a shmirshky's life when her period stops.* The term *menopause* is often casually used in reference to the perimenopause experience; however, technically, menopause is the point in time when a shmirshky has been without her period for twelve consecutive months. http://www.nlm.nih.gov/medlineplus/menopause.html http://www.menopause.org/Portals/0/Content/PDF/A.pdf	10
natural hormone	A hormone originally derived from a plant or animal source.	67
osteoporosis	A medical condition in which the bones become brittle, typically as a result of a hormonal deficiency or reduced calcium or vitamin D levels. Shmirshkies in PM&M experience a decrease in estrogen, which can contribute to osteoporosis. http://www.nlm.nih.gov/medlineplus/ency/article/000360.htm	59

---

* Unfortunately, the technical definitions of premature menopause, premenopause, perimenopause, menopause, and postmenopause rarely do justice to the actual PM&M experience. The process takes years and years to go through, and each shmirshky has different symptoms and stories. After reading this book—and living through PM&M—you can write your own definitions!

Term	Definition	Page
Pap smear	An examination of cells scraped from the cervix. This sampling is then examined under a microscope by a pathologist to determine if any of the cells are cancerous or precancerous. http://www.nlm.nih.gov/medlineplus/ency/article/003911.htm	57
perimenopause	A time in a shmirshky's life that no one ever mentioned to me, probably because I would have requested a sex change immediately. Typically, perimenopause is the six- to ten-year symptom-laden span of time before a shmirshky finally stops getting her period for twelve consecutive months. Often when people say, "I'm going through menopause," they are describing the perimenopausal part of the journey. http://www.menopause.org/glossary.aspx	10

Term	Definition	Page
PMS	Premenstrual syndrome; the symptoms that shmirshkies often get before their period arrives. Symptoms may include bloating, constipation, cravings, sore breasts, headache, and feeling unusually emotional, irritable, tired, anxious, or depressed, just to name a few. (Sounds like fun, right?) http://www.nlm.nih.gov/medlineplus/ency/article/001505.htm	7
postmenopause	Yet another time in a shmirshky's life that is not discussed. Post-menopause begins about five years after a shmirshky has reached the point of menopause and continues throughout the rest of her life. A shmirshky in post-menopause typically would have permanently reduced hormone levels. I'm not quite there yet, but I am hoping postmenopause won't involve any postgraduate work. http://www.menopause.org/Portals/0/Content/PDF/A.pdf	10

Term	Definition	Page
Premarin	A hormone replacement made from the urine of pregnant horses, which was reported on in the 2002 Women's Health Initiative studies. http://www.drugs.com/premarin.html	70
premature menopause	Most shmirshkies begin to experience PM&M symptoms in their forties or fifties. Early PM&M storms can also occur for some shmirshkies. If a shmirshky's period is gone for twelve consecutive months or more, before the age of forty, this is currently known as premature menopause. Many resources say premature menopause can be a result of one's genetic makeup, an illness, or medical procedures; however, some restrict it to only natural (nonsurgical) causes. http://www.menopause.org/Portals/0/Content/PDF/A.pdf	9
premenopause	This is a confusing and sort of antiquated term that is generally being phased out. Technically, premenopause means the entire time in a shmirshky's life before menopause, but that is a bit too broad to be useful. http://www.menopause.org/Portals/0/Content/PDF/A.pdf	9

Term	Definition	Page
progesterone	The hormone that stimulates the uterus and gets it ready for pregnancy. Progesterone also regulates the monthly menstrual cycle. Low levels of progesterone can impact your mood and cause irritability, among other things. http://www.nlm.nih.gov/medlineplus/ menopause.html http://www.medterms.com/script/main/ art.asp?articlekey=5060	62
Progestin	A nonbioidentical form of HRT, intended to supplement low levels of progesterone in the body. http://www.thefreedictionary.com/ progestin	159
Provera	A synthetic progesterone included in the 2002 Women's Health Initiative studies. http://www.drugs.com/pdr/provera.html	70
synthetic hormone	A hormone whose chemical structure has been altered in a laboratory.	67
synthroid	Medication commonly used to treat hypothyroidism.	85

Term	Definition	Page
T3 and T4	Thyroid hormones that get released into the bloodstream and control the body's metabolism. The 3 and the 4 refer to the number of iodine molecules in that form of the hormone. http://www.endocrineweb.com/ thyfunction.html	34, 63
testosterone (free and total)	Free testosterone is the unbound, metabolically active testosterone. Total testosterone includes both the free and bound testosterone. In shmirshkies, the ovaries produce testosterone. This benefits shmirshkies by helping to maintain a healthy libido, strong bones, muscle mass, and mental stability. http://www.medterms.com/script/main/ art.asp?articlekey=5747	61
thyroid condition	A condition that affects the thyroid gland, such as hyperthyroidism, hypothyroidism, and others. http://www.endocrineweb.com/thy function.html	33
thyroid gland	A small, two-lobed gland in your neck that uses iodine to make thyroid hormones that help regulate your metabolism. http://www.endocrineweb.com/ thyfunction.html	33

Term	Definition	Page
triglycerides	Molecules of fatty acid produced in your body and from foods, which are stored in fat cells in your body. http://www.nlm.nih.gov/medlineplus/ency/article/003493.htm	60
TSH	Thyroid stimulating hormone. An imbalance in your TSH levels is one of the main indicators of a thyroid condition. http://www.nlm.nih.gov/medlineplus/ency/article/003684.htm	34
Type A	Type A people are known for their impatience, aggressiveness, and competitiveness. http://stress.about.com/od/understandingstress/a/type_a_person.htm	102
Type B	Type B folks are known for having a lack of aggressiveness and tension. http://www.answers.com/topic/type-b-personality	102
ultrasound scan	Ultrasound uses high-frequency sound waves to take pictures of the internal systems of the body. There is no exposure to radiation. You don't feel a thing! http://www.nlm.nih.gov/medlineplus/ency/article/003336.htm	36

Term	Definition	Page
Vitamin D3	This vitamin, named after my husband's first initial, is typically absorbed from sunlight through the skin. D3 helps to maintain normal blood levels of calcium and phosphorus, and helps keep your bones nice and strong. http://www.nlm.nih.gov/medlineplus/druginfo/natural/patient-vitamind.html	64
WHI	The Women's Health Initiative, which was created by the National Heart, Lung, and Blood Institute, a division of the National Institutes of Health under the U.S. Department of Health and Human Services. The WHI conducted a series of clinical trials and observational studies on postmenopausal shmirshkies. http://www.nhlbi.nih.gov/whi	69

hormone therapy menu

✳ Oral or tablet form: This is the most common type of hormone therapy. When swallowed, the medication *immediately* travels to the liver (via the gastrointestinal tract), where the majority of the hormone is metabolized (deactivated); then a small fraction of active hormone goes into the bloodstream.

✳ Patches: These are applied to your skin below your waist—for example, on your stomach, thigh, bottom, or hip (swab the area with alcohol first, and the patch will stick better). Patches need to be changed once or twice a week depending on your prescription and your needs. It is best to place them in a different location each time to prevent skin irritation.

✳ Implants: These are small pellets that are inserted into the fat under the skin. This process is carried out with a local anesthetic in your doctor's office. These implants last about four to six months.

✳ Transdermal creams, gels, and sprays: These can be applied to the skin, usually once or twice daily. After application, the medication is absorbed into the bloodstream.

✳ Vaginal treatments: These come as tablets or creams that are inserted into the shmirshky, similar to a suppository.

They can help to ease vaginal discomfort. There is also a vaginal ring available, which can be left in the shmirshky for three months. It slowly releases estradiol (the most potent form of the three natural estrogens) into the vaginal tissues. Estriol, the weakest form of estrogen, can also be applied into the shmirshky in the form of vaginal creams. It may ease frequent urination or urgency and painful intercourse.

✳ Sublingual: These are liquids or tablets. At present, these are only available from compounding pharmacies.*

Patches, implants, gels, creams, sprays, and sublingual methods all transmit hormones to your body first through your bloodstream, making a first pass to their sites of action and then ultimately degrading in the liver. Because these methods do not go directly through the gastrointestinal tract, you can keep the dose much lower than with the oral or tablet form.

---

* Compounding pharmacies create medication formulas, specifically designed for a particular individual's needs.

hormone therapy brands*

Estrogen

Brand (hormone)	Bioidentical	Application
Alora (estradiol)	X	generic cream, gel, pill (oral), patch
Bi-est (estradiol, estriol)	X	generic cream, gel, pill
Cenestin (conjugated estrogens)		pill
Climara (estradiol)	X	patch
Delestrogen (estradiol valerate)		injection
Depo-Estradiol (estradiol cypionate)		injection

* Information for this section was gathered from http://www.pdr.net and through the help of my pharmacist and doctors. These hormone therapy options were all available as of September 1, 2010. As you know, many new drugs come on the market each day, and some get taken off. Since I am not a doctor, I can't recommend or suggest any of these drugs. If you choose to try hormone therapy, it is critical to find the right doctor to be your partner and help you make the right choices.

I've indicated which of these hormone therapy options are bioidentical or not for quick and easy reference, but this should by no means be the only factor you consider when going on hormone therapy. If your doctor prescribes HRT, discuss all the different options and learn as much as you can about the medicine that he or she suggests so that you are comfortable with what you put into your body.

For the purposes of this chart, hormone therapy options that contain a bioidentical hormone as well as a nonbioidentical hormone all wrapped up into the same medicine are classified as nonbioidentical, since you can't separate the bioidentical hormone from the nonbioidentical hormone before the medicine is administered.

Estrogen (continued)

Brand (hormone)	Bioidentical	Application
Divigel (estradiol)	X	gel
Elestrin (estradiol)	X	gel
Enjuvia (conjugated estrogens)		pill
Esclim (estradiol)	X	patch
Estrace (estradiol)	X	cream, pill
Estraderm (estradiol)	X	patch
Estradiol (estradiol)	X	various generics, compounded implant, cream, capsule, suppository
Estrasorb (estradiol)	X	gel
Estring (estradiol)	X	vaginal ring
EstroGel (estradiol)	X	gel
Evamist (estradiol)	X	transdermal spray
Femring (estradiol acetate)		vaginal ring
Femtrace (estradiol acetate)		pill
Gynodiol (estradiol)	X	pill
Innofem (estradiol)	X	pill
Menest (esterified estrogens)		pill
Menostar (estradiol)	X	gel
Ogen (estropipate)		cream, pill
Ortho-Est (estropipate)		pill

Estrogen (continued)

Brand (hormone)	Bioidentical	Application
Premarin (conjugated estrogens)		cream, pill
Tri-est (estrone, estradiol, estriol)	X	generic and compounded cream, gel, pill
Vagifem (estradiol)	X	vaginal tablet
Vivelle (estradiol)	X	patch
Vivelle-Dot (estradiol)	X	patch

Progesterone

Brand (hormone)	Bioidentical	Application
Crinone (progesterone)	X	vaginal gel
Endometrim (progesterone)	X	vaginal insert
Prochieve (progesterone)	X	vaginal gel
Progesterone (progesterone)	X	generic and compounded cream, gel, suppository, capsule, injection
Prometrium (progesterone)	X	pill, capsule
Provera (medroxyprogesterone acetate)		pill, capsule

Testosterone

Brand (hormone)	Bioidentical	Application
Androderm (testosterone)	X	gel
AndroGel (testosterone)	X	cream
Delatestryl (testosterone enanthate)		injection
Depo-Testosterone (testosterone cypionate)		injection
Striant (testosterone)	X	buccal tablet
Testim (testosterone)	X	gel
Testosterone (testosterone)	X	various generics and compounded cream, implant, gel, injection, and cream
Testred (methyltestosterone)		various generics, compounded pill, sublingual tablet

Combination Estrogen/Progestin*

Brand (hormone)	Bioidentical	Application
Activella (estradiol, norethindrone acetate)		pill
Angeliq (drospirenone, estradiol)		pill
Climara-Pro (estradiol, levonorgestrel)		patch

* Progestin is a nonbioidentical form of HRT intended to supplement low levels of progesterone in the body.

Combination Estrogen/Progestin (continued)

Brand (hormone)	Bioidentical	Application
CombiPatch (estradiol, norethindrone acetate)		patch
FemHRT (ethinyl estradiol, norethindrone acetate)		pill
Prefest (estradiol, norgestimate)		pill
Premphase (conjugated estrogens, medroxyprogesterone acetate)		pill
Prempro (conjugated estrogens, medroxyprogesterone acetate)		pill

Combination Estrogen/Testosterone

Brand (hormone)	Bioidentical	Application
Covaryx (esterified estrogens, methyltestosterone)		pill
Covaryx HS (esterified estrogens, methyltestosterone)		pill
Essian (esterified estrogens, methyltestosterone)		pill
Essian HS (esterified estrogens, methyltestosterone)		pill
Estratest (esterified estrogens, methyltestosterone)		pill
Estratest HS (esterified estrogens, methyltestosterone)		pill

resources and notes

Menopause and Shmirshky Health

"The Endangered Uterus" by Peg Rosen
http://www.more.com/4488/2382-the-endangered-uterus

FDA: For Women
http://www.fda.gov/womens

GynEndo News
http://www.gynendonews.com

Healthfinder.gov
http://www.healthfinder.gov/scripts/SearchContext.asp?topic=541

Mayo Clinic
http://www.mayoclinic.com/health/menopause/DS00119

Medline Plus: Women's Health
http://www.nlm.nih.gov/medlineplus/womenshealth.html

North American Menopause Society (NAMS)
http://www.menopause.org

Project AWARE (Association of Women for the Advancement of Research and Education)
http://www.project-aware.org/Experience/premature.shtml

Shmirshky.com
http://www.shmirshky.com

WHI Publications: Hormone Therapy
http://www.nhlbi.nih.gov/whi/references.htm#ht

Women's Health Initiative (WHI)
http://www.nhlbi.nih.gov/whi

Women's Healthcare Forum
http://www.womenshealthcareforum.com/menopause.cfm

Menopause and Shmirshky Health (continued)

Your Total Health: Hormone Replacement Therapy
http://yourtotalhealth.ivillage.com/hormone-replacement-therapy.html?
   pageNum=1

General Health

Harvard Medical School
http://hms.harvard.edu/hms/home.asp

HealthGrades
http://www.healthgrades.com

Mayo Clinic
http://www.mayoclinic.com

Medline Plus: Medical Encyclopedia
http://www.nlm.nih.gov/medlineplus/encyclopedia.html

University of Colorado Denver Anschutz Medical Campus
http://www.ucdenver.edu/about/denver/Pages/
   AnschutzMedicalCampus.aspx

Thyroid Information

About.com: Thyroid Disease
http://thyroid.about.com/library/links/blthyroid.htm

American Association of Clinical Endocrinologists
http://www.aace.com

American Thyroid Association
http://www.thyroid.org

Endocrine Society
http://www.endo-society.org

EndocrineWeb
http://www.endocrineweb.com

Thyroid Information (continued)

EndocrineWeb: How Your Thyroid Works
http://www.endocrineweb.com/thyfunction.html

Parathyroid.com
http://www.parathyroid.com

Thyroid-info.com
http://www.thyroid-info.com

Thyroid Power
http://www.thyroidpower.com

Researching Doctors and Pharmacies

American Board of Medical Specialties
(the service is free, but registration is required)
https://www.abms.org/WC/login.aspx

American Medical Association
http://www.ama-assn.org/ama/pub/education-careers/
    becoming-physician/medical-licensure/state-medical-boards.shtml

International Academy of Compounding Pharmacists
http://www.iacprx.org

National Association of Boards of Pharmacy
http://www.nabp.net/

RateMDs
http://www.ratemds.com/social

Acupuncture and Alternative Medicine

American Academy of Medical Acupuncture Referral Search
http://www.medicalacupuncture.org/findadoc/index.html

National Institutes of Health: National Center for Complementary
and Alternative Medicine
http://nccam.nih.gov/health/acupuncture/introduction.htm

Acupuncture and Alternative Medicine (continued)

State-by-state acupuncture certification requirements
http://www.acupuncture.com/statelaws/statelaw.htm

Information on Clinical Drug Trials

CenterWatch
http://www.centerwatch.com

National Institutes of Health: ClinicalTrials.gov
http://www.clinicaltrials.gov

Women's Health Initiative: Participant Web site
http://www.whi.org

Other Helpful Links

Association of Sewing and Design Professionals
http://www.paccprofessionals.org

Find a Dressmaker
http://www.findadressmaker.com/list.html

Shmirshky.com
http://www.shmirshky.com

Spanx
http://www.spanx.com

additional notes

All Web sites mentioned in the book were last retrieved on October 9, 2010, unless otherwise specified. All sources cited in the book are found in the Shmirshky Not-So-Fun Terms, which correspond to specific points in the text and footnotes, except for the following citations:

meet the shmirshky
For the number of shmirshkies in M from page 2, see Mary Shomon, "Thyroid Problems and Menopause," Thyroid-info.com: http://www.thyroid-info.com/articles/menopause.htm

CHAPTER 8, sleepless in PM&M
For the complete University of Arizona College of Nursing study on PM&M symptoms by Berg, Larson, and Pasvogel, see the *Journal of Clinical Nursing*:
http://onlinelibrary.wiley.com/doi/10.1111/j.1365-2702.2007.02112.x/full

CHAPTER 9, the thyroidian slip
There is a footnote about Hashimoto's disease on page 34. For the statistics on hypothyroidism, see Mary Shomon, "The Thyroid/ Menopause Connection: Information from Richard and Karilee Shames," Thyroid-info.com:
http://www.thyroid-info.com/articles/shamesmenopause.htm

There is a footnote about the treatability of thyroid cancer on page 37. For more information, see MedlinePlus: Medical Encyclopedia,"Thyroid Cancer":

http://www.nlm.nih.gov/medlineplus/ency/article/001213.htm

CHAPTER 14, shmirshky numbers
The suggested ranges for Total cholesterol, HDL, LDL, and Triglycerides on page 60 are explained further in the American Heart Association's "What Your Cholesterol Levels Mean":
http://www.heart.org/HEARTORG/Conditions/Cholesterol/AboutCholesterol/What-Your-Cholesterol-Levels-Mean UCM 305562 Article.jsp

The cholesterol/HDL range on page 60 is explained further in Lab Tests Online, "HDL Cholesterol: The Test":
http://www.labtestsonline.org/understanding/analytes/hdl/test.html

The suggested range for TSH on page 63 is explained further in American Association of Clinical Endocrinologists, "Thyroid Awareness Month Tip Sheet":
http://www.aace.com/public/awareness/tam/2006/pdfs/TAMTipSheet.pdf

For more on the discrepancy between various recommended TSH levels on page 63, see Mayo Clinic, "Subclinical Hypothyroidism: An Update for Primary Care Physicians":
http://www.mayoclinicproceedings.com/content/84/1/65.full

The suggested range for Vitamin D on page 64 is explained further in:
http://orthoinfo.aaos.org/topic.cfm?topic=A00567

For additional information about PM&M and Vitamin D3, see "Vitamin D—Overhyped or Underused" by Ginny Graves: http://www.more.com/2030/24164-vitamin-d-overhyped-or-underused

CHAPTER 15, **to hrt or not to hrt?**
The definition of estrogen dominance came from Dr. Margery Gass, Executive Director, The North American Menopause Society. The NAMS's own "Menopause Glossary" can be found at http://www.menopause.org/glossary.aspx

CHAPTER 20, **shmirshky redecorated**
For more on hysterectomies from pages 89 and 90, see Peg Rosen, "The Endangered Uterus," *More Magazine* (December 2008/ January 2009): http://www.more.com/4488/2382-the-endangered-uterus

Shmirshky Daily Symptoms Chart

How Hot Are Your Symptoms?

S – small problem
M – medium problem
L – large problem
Blank square – not a problem

_____
month / year

_____
name

_____
birthday

day of the month

period
spotting, light, typical, heavy

mental/emotional
memory lapses (sticky notes aplenty)
overly sensitive
uncontrollable crying
unusually depressed and withdrawn
overall sense that I'm not OK
tense (like a rubber band ready to snap)
overwhelmed
anxious
irritable
bursts of anger
violent
low sex drive

1 2 3 4 5 6 7 8 9 10 11 12 13 14 15 16 17 18 19 20 21 22 23 24 25 26 27 28 29 30 31

This chart is designed to be a symptoms guide for PM&M shmirshkies. Fill out the chart every day and share it with your PM&M doctor as part of your overall medical assessment. This will make it easier for your doctor to target your individual needs.

© 2010 Shmirshky Universal. All rights reserved. SHMIRSHKY, THINK INSIDE THE BOX, THE PURSUIT OF HORMONE HAPPINESS, PM&M, SUMO FREE, ERLICK, FF, and all other logos are trademarks of Shmirshky Universal.

physical	oddly dry skin	headaches/migraines	exhausted	hair loss	pms-like bloating	sore or ballooning breasts	increased chin whiskers	deepening voice	pimples galore	hot flashes or flushes	night drenches	sleepless nights	heart palpitations	weight gain (shrinking pants)	stiffness, aches, and pains	bladder issues	shmirshky infections	excessive shmirshky discharge	breakthrough shmirshky bleeding	dry shmirshky (sex hurts)	harder to reach orgasm	other joys of PM&M				
1																						1				
2																						2				
3																						3				
4																						4				
5																						5				
6																						6				
7																						7				
8																						8				
9																						9				
10																						10				
11																						11				
12																						12				
13																						13				
14																						14				
15																						15				
16																						16				
17																						17				
18																						18				
19																						19				
20																						20				
21																						21				
22																						22				
23																						23				
24																						24				
25																						25				
26																						26				
27																						27				
28																						28				
29																						29				
30																						30				
31																						31				

my shmirshky journal

PM&M feels like . . .

Dearest You,

Let me be the first to welcome you to the shmirshky movement! Shmirshky is all about reaching out, so come chat and party with me at **shmirshky.com.**

You can find support on the message board, get the lastest shmirshky blogs and PM&M news, and find great tips on how to host a Shmirshky Party!

The shmirshky community wants to hear from you, so keep us posted about your life and how you're feeling.

Remember, reaching out is IN. Suffering in silence is OUT!

Hugs,
E